Time for MENTALS

Paul
Nightingale

5

Book 5

HUNTER
EDUCATION
NIGHTINGALE

Copyright © 2015 Paul Nightingale
Time for Mentals - Book 5

Published by:
Hunter Education Nightingale
ABN: 69 055 798 626
PO Box 547
Warners Bay NSW 2282
Ph: 0417 658 777
email: sales@huntereducationnightingale.com.au
        paul@huntereducationnightingale.com.au
        www.huntereducationnightingale.com.au

Cover Design: Brooke Lewis

National Library of Australia Card No.
and ISBN 978 - 1 - 922242 - 13 - 6

RECYCLING

When the program is completed and the paper no longer wanted, be sure to have it recycled. The time and care taken to recycle may help save a tree and maintain our environment.

E	D	C	B	A
19	18	17	16	15

ime for Mentals

ook 5

bout this Book

he for Mentals - Year 5 is the sixth in a series seven books that addresses the Year 5 Level scriptions and sections of the new Mathematics riculum. This book reinforces the concept and ivities introduced in the strands found in its rfect partner Time for Maths - Year 5. The book also be used for homework or extension.

hen this book is used in parallel with Time for aths - Year 5, a solid meaningful understanding Number and Place Value, Patterns and Algebra, ing Units of Measurement along with interpreting d representing data will be achieved by the ld. In addition the child will learn the language mathematics so the processes and concepts come more enriching as he/she moves from unit unit.

Time for Mentals - Year 5 contains 28 self contained units, each of four sections. Answers to all activities are provided at the end of the book for the teacher or parent. This support and knowledge will help the child develop understanding and build confidence with mathematics.

While the book is a valuable extension, reinforcement and builder of mathematics skills in the classroom, it is also an ideal learning tool for use at home.

Message to Parents

A child using Time for Mentals - Year 5 helps develop an understanding of mathematical concepts - a parent should resist the temptation to actually provide answers but support and assist when necessary.

As a parent you help your child learn everyday. This book provides activities to help develop concepts, processes and proficiencies needed for the development of mathematics, which parents can assist with as the child moves from unit to unit.

At all times encourage and praise each units performance by the child. Help by checking answers, but remember the understanding of mathematical concepts develop over time with practice.

Enjoy, encourage and praise your child's work at home as he/she moves towards mastering the proficiencies and understanding of mathematics. This book provides activities to enable parents to help develop the child's concepts, processes and skills.

Division

1. Convert each number sentence to a formal operation and then write the answer.

a. $30 \div 3 =$ ☐

b. $27 \div 3 =$ ☐

c. $48 \div 6 =$ ☐

d. $32 \div 4 =$ ☐

2. Write the improper fraction as a completed number sentence.

a. $\dfrac{28}{4} =$ ☐ $\div$ ☐ $=$ ☐

b. $\dfrac{39}{3} =$ ☐ $\div$ ☐ $=$ ☐

c. $\dfrac{24}{6} =$ ☐ $\div$ ☐ $=$ ☐

3. Complete each division operation.

a. $6\overline{)30}$ b. $8\overline{)64}$ c. $9\overline{)36}$

d. $7\overline{)42}$ e. $5\overline{)55}$ f. $4\overline{)48}$

4. a. How many times can 5 go into 40? ☐

   b. Divide 35 by 7 ☐

   c. 64 socks, how many pairs? ☐

   d. How many 8s in 56? ☐

Decimal Fractions

1. Write the decimal fraction for the coloured part of each set of squares.

a. ☐☐☐☐☐☐☐☐☐☐ =

b. ☐☐☐☐☐☐☐☐☐☐ =

c. ☐☐☐☐☐☐☐☐☐☐ =

d. ☐☐☐☐☐☐☐☐☐☐ =

2. Write each decimal fraction in tenths.

a. $0.7 = \dfrac{\square}{10}$ b. $0.3 = \dfrac{\square}{10}$ c. $0.9 = \dfrac{\square}{1}$

d. $0.2 = \dfrac{\square}{10}$ e. $0.6 = \dfrac{\square}{10}$ f. $0.5 = \dfrac{\square}{1}$

g. $0.4 = \dfrac{\square}{10}$ h. $0.1 = \dfrac{\square}{10}$ $\dfrac{?}{10}$

3. Write the fraction missing from each table.

	Fraction	Decimal		Fraction	Decim
a.	$\dfrac{1}{2}$		b.	$\dfrac{9}{10}$	
c.	$\dfrac{3}{10}$		d.		0.2
e.		0.7	f.	$\dfrac{1}{4}$	
g.	$\dfrac{4}{5}$		h.		0.6

4. Colour the squares to show each fraction.

a. $\dfrac{1}{2}$ ☐☐☐☐☐☐☐☐☐☐

b. $\dfrac{6}{10}$ ☐☐☐☐☐☐☐☐☐☐

c. $\dfrac{8}{10}$ ☐☐☐☐☐☐☐☐☐☐

d. $\dfrac{3}{10}$ ☐☐☐☐☐☐☐☐☐☐

e. $\dfrac{1}{5}$ ☐☐☐☐☐☐☐☐☐☐

Length

Shopping

Write each measurement in decimal notation.

a. 300 cm _____ m **b.** 258 cm _____ m

c. 750 cm _____ m **d.** 172 cm _____ m

e. 1 360 cm _____ m **f.** 12 300 cm _____ m

Draw the length of each line down the page

a. 4 cm   **b.** 6 cm   **c.** 3 ½ cm

Use a ruler to measure the perimeter of each shape.

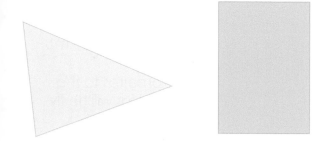

rimeter = ☐ cm   Perimeter = ☐ cm

Write the unit - centimetres (cm), millimetres (mm), or metres (m) for each item.

a. length of a pen _____

b. length of a stamp _____

c. length of the kitchen _____

d. length of your eye lashes _____

e. perimeter of this book _____

1. How much will you spend to buy all of these items?

$2.47 $3.62 $4.89

$2.49 $4.72 $2.70

$ ☐

2. How much will you pay for 4 books if one book costs $15? $ ☐

3. Paris saves $8 each week. How much will she have in ten weeks? $ ☐

4. What change will you get from $100 if you buy these items?

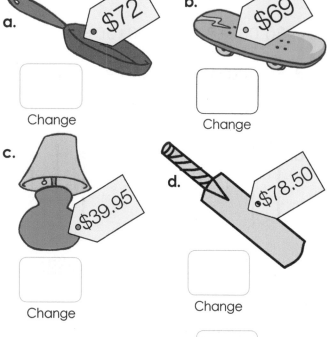

a. $72   **b.** $69

☐ Change   ☐ Change

c. $39.95   **d.** $78.50

☐ Change   ☐ Change

5. How many $5 in $170? $ ☐

6. How many 50 cents in $120? $ ☐

Place Value

1. Write the number represented on each place value card.

a.

TTH	TH	H	T	O

_____

b.

TTH	TH	H	T	O

_____

c.

TTH	TH	H	T	O

_____

2. Write the place value for each circled number.

a. 8 ③ 2 4 1 _____

b. 7 5 ① 6 7 _____

c. ③ 8 5 2 9 _____

d. 5 6 ⑦ 4 5 _____

3. Write the whole number for each expanded number.

a. 60 000+4 000+200+70+6= _____

b. 70 000+2 000+900+40+2= _____

c. 30 000+8 000+700+50+1= _____

d. 90 000+2 000+60+7= _____

4. Write the number showing on each abacus.

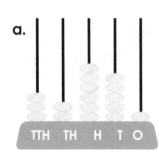

a. TTH TH H T O

b. TTH TH H T O

_____   _____

5. Write 27 386 in words.

_____

6 _____

Multiplication

1. Write each multiplication number sentence as an algorithm.

a. 1 232 x 2 =

TH	H	T	
X			

b. 3 122 x 3 =

TH	H	T	
X			

c. 1 222 x 4 =

TH	H	T	
X			

2. Write the answer for each algorithm.

a. 12
  x 4
____

b. 15
  x 3
____

c. 18
  x 5
____

d. 1
  x
____

3. a. A glass holds 375 mL of water. How much will 2 glasses hold?

375 x 2 =_____ mL

b. Dad flies 2 465 kilometres to the mine for work. How far will he fly there and back?

2 465 x ☐ _____ km
=

4.

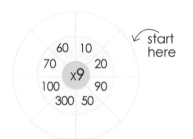

60 10
70 ×9 20
100 90
300 50

↙ start here

5. Write the product of these numbers.

a. 7 and 12 = ☐   **b.** 9 and 4 = ☐

c. 6 and 20 = ☐   **d.** 5 and 15 = ☐

Area

Count the one and the half centimetre squares to find the area of each shape.

i.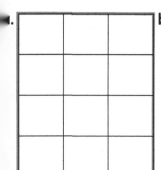

b.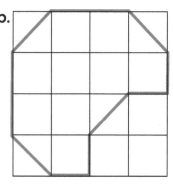

Area = ☐ cm²   Area = ☐ cm²

Write the appropriate unit of area in cm² or m² for each object.

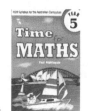
a.

b.

600 _____   375 _____

d.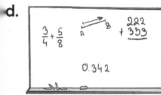

c.

2 _____

e.

3.75 _____

150 _____

Use the measurement of each shape to write its area.

	Length	Width	Area
a.	6 cm	5 cm	cm²
b.	7 cm	3 cm	cm²
c.	8 cm	4 cm	cm²
d.	5 cm	12 cm	cm²

Write the area of this stamp.

2 cm

3 cm   Area = _____

Time

1. Write each time in 24 hour time.

   a. 6:30 am _____   **b.** 7:45 pm _____

   c. 8:20 pm _____   **d.** 9:15 am _____

   e. 4:40 pm _____   **f.** 3:50 pm _____

2. Write each pm time in 24 hour format.

   a.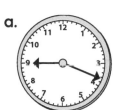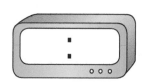

   b.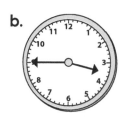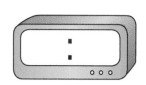

   c.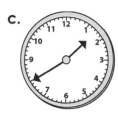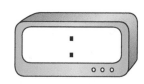

   d.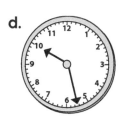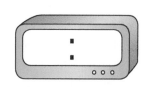

   e.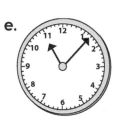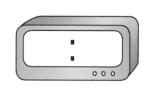

3. Write each time as am or pm time.

   a. 2000 _____   **b.** 1645 _____

   c. 1756 _____   **d.** 2340 _____

   e. 1445 _____   **f.** 1327 _____

   g. 0856 _____   **h.** 0642 _____

Subtraction

1. Find the difference without trading, for these numbers.

a. 725 - 312 = ☐

b. 869 - 314 = ☐

c. 657 - 223 = ☐

d. 489 - 267 = ☐

2. Find the difference using trading, with tens and ones.

a.

TH	H	T	O
8	3	5	4
− 5	1	2	7

b.

TH	H	T	O
7	8	7	3
− 2	1	4	8

c.

TH	H	T	O
8	5	7	2
− 3	3	1	9

d.

TH	H	T	O
6	9	5	0
− 4	3	1	4

3. Farmer Brown had 7 385 sheep to shear. At the end of the week he still had 2 129 sheep to shear. How many had he shorn?

TH	H	T	O
−			

_____ sheep had been shorn.

4. Take the numbers down the side from those across the top.

a.	−	81	292	174	283	870	465
b.	28						
c.	47						
d.	36						

8

Percentages

1. Write each fraction as a percentage.

a. $\frac{72}{100} =$ _____ %

b. $\frac{53}{100} =$ _____

c. $\frac{38}{100} =$ _____ %

d. $\frac{24}{100} =$ _____

e. 0.77 = _____ %

f. 0.2 = _____

g. 0.36 = _____ %

h. $\frac{4}{10} =$ _____

2. Write the percentage for the shaded part on each hundredth grid.

a.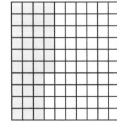

_____ %

b.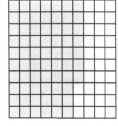

_____ %

c.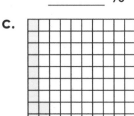

_____ %

d.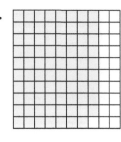

_____ %

3. Change each decimal to a percentage.

a. 0.74 = _____ %

b. 0.85 = _____

c. 0.32 = _____ %

d. 0.68 = _____

e. 0.06 = _____ %

f. 0.50 = _____

4. Complete the table below.

	Fraction	Decimal	Percentage
a.	$\frac{3}{4}$		
b.		0.4	
c.			32%
d.	$\frac{9}{10}$		
e.		0.25	

Volume

Count the centicubes in each shape.

a.

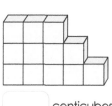

[ ] centicubes

b.

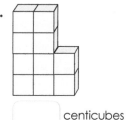

[ ] centicubes

c.

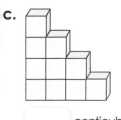

[ ] centicubes

d.

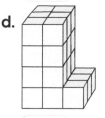

[ ] centicubes

The volume of a regular prism can be found by multiplying length by width by the height. The unit for volume is either m³ or cm³.

L x W x H = volume
4 x 2 x 3 = 24 cm³   3 H 2 W 4 L

Find the volume of each shape by multiplying L x W x H = volume³.

a.

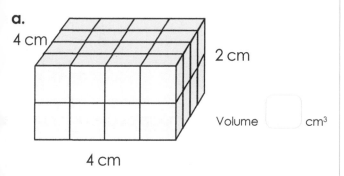

4 cm
2 cm
4 cm

Volume [ ] cm³

b.

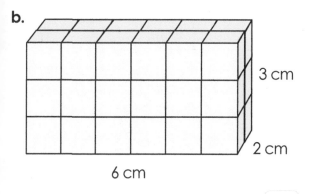

3 cm
2 cm
6 cm

Volume [ ] cm³

Probabilities

1. On a scale of 0 to 1 rate the chance of each event happening. Use this scale.

| 0 | 0.1 | 0.2 | 0.3 | 0.4 | 0.5 | 0.6 | 0.7 | 0.8 | 0.9 | 1 |

Never happen   50-50 chance   certain to happen

a. Mum will win lotto tonight. _____

b. My birthday is in May. _____

c. A tail will turn up on a coin toss. _____

d. It will rain tomorrow. _____

e. Birds fly north in winter. _____

f. The postie will bring mail today _____

2. Rate the chance or probability of the spinner landing on each colour. Yellow is done for you.

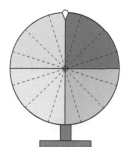

a. yellow 0.25

b. blue _____

c. green _____

d. red _____

3. On which spinner would you rate a 1 for red? [ ]

a.
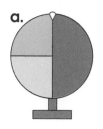

b.
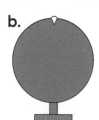

c.
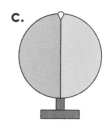

4. On which spinner would you rate a 0 for red? [ ]

5. List 2 events that could happen today.

1._____

2._____

6. How many rolls of a die did it take you to roll a 5? [ ]

9

Addition

1. Add each group of numbers to find the total.

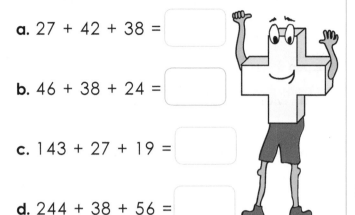

a. 27 + 42 + 38 = ⬜

b. 46 + 38 + 24 = ⬜

c. 143 + 27 + 19 = ⬜

d. 244 + 38 + 56 = ⬜

2. Add the four-digit numbers using trading with tens and ones.

a.
TH	H	T	O
	6	3	2	6
+	2	3	3	9

b.
TH	H	T	O
	4	1	7	8
+	3	5	1	7

c.
TH	H	T	O
	1	3	7	6
+	5	3	1	6

d.
TH	H	T	O
	5	1	6	5
+	3	2	7	8

3. Add across and down to complete the addition grid.

+	8	3	12	7	
5	9	3	16		a.
27	41	18	37		b.
					c.
					d.

4. Add the odd numbers less than 20. ⬜

5. Add the product of 8 and 7 plus 63. ⬜

6. Write the sum of 203, 185, 722 and 64. ⬜

10 7. ⬜ + 5 235 = 7 456.

Factors and Multiples

1. Write the factors for each number.

a. 12 _____, _____, _____, _____, _____, —

b. 15 _____, _____, _____, _____,

c. 20 _____, _____, _____, _____, _____, —

d. 39 _____, _____, _____, _____,

2. Answer True (T) or False (F) to these.

a. 8 is a factor of 24 _____

b. 27 is a factor of 81 _____

c. 17 is a factor of 51 _____

d. 7 is a factor of 27 _____

3. Colour the multiples for each number.

a.
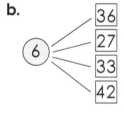

b.
	36
6	27
	33
	42

c.
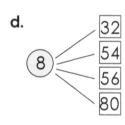

d.
	32
8	54
	56
	80

4. Write the first five multiples of each number.

a. 3 ⬜, ⬜, ⬜, ⬜, ⬜

b. 7 ⬜, ⬜, ⬜, ⬜, ⬜

c. 5 ⬜, ⬜, ⬜, ⬜, ⬜

d. 9 ⬜, ⬜, ⬜, ⬜, ⬜

e. 4 ⬜, ⬜, ⬜, ⬜, ⬜

Capacity

How many millilitres in these?

a. 3.5 L _____ mL **b.** $\frac{1}{2}$ L _____ mL

c. 1 Litre _____ mL **d.** $2\frac{1}{4}$ L _____ mL

e. 2.5 L _____ mL **f.** $5\frac{1}{4}$ L _____ mL

What capacity level is showing on each cylinder?

a. 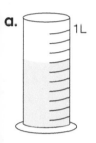 **b.** 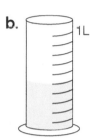 **c.**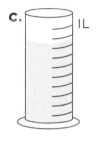

_____ mL _____ mL _____ mL

Use the following objects to find the capacity of each group of containers.

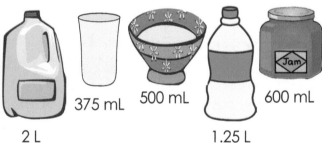

375 mL 500 mL 600 mL

2 L 1.25 L

a.  Capacity = _____

b.  Capacity = _____

Write the millilitres in decimal form.

a. 375 mL _____ **b.** 600 mL _____

c. 400 mL _____ **d.** 750 mL _____

e. 250mL _____ **f.** 1 350 mL _____

Location

1. Write the co-ordinates for each shape marked on the grid.

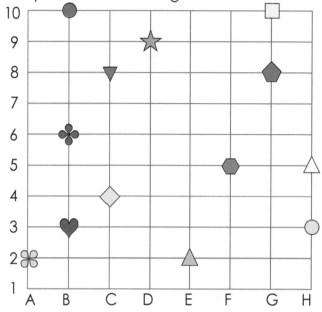

1. ● _____ 6. ▢ _____

2. ◇ _____ 7. ✿ _____

3. ★ _____ 8. △ _____

4. ▲ _____ 9. ○ _____

5. ✿ _____ 10. ▼ _____

2. Give the co-ordinates for each lettered square.

	A	B	C	D	E	F
5	Ø		V	F		D
4		A		Z		
3	M				B	
2			C			Y
1	E				X	

a. A _____ **b.** D _____

c. B _____ **d.** E _____

e. C _____ **f.** F _____

g. X _____ **h.** Y _____

i. Z _____ **j.** Ø _____

k. M _____ **l.** V _____

11

Rounding Off

1. Round off each number to the nearest 10.

a. 78 _____ **b.** 96 _____ **c.** 54 _____

d. 82 _____ **e.** 27 _____ **f.** 41 _____

g. 53 _____ **h.** 19 _____ **i.** 88 _____

2. Round off each sum of money to the nearest five cents.

a. $ 2.37 _____ **b.** $ 4.98 _____

c. $ 10.46 _____ **d.** $ 7.22 _____

e. $ 12.54 _____ **f.** $ 8.78 _____

3. Round off each number to the nearest thousand.

a. 8 216 _____ **b.** 5 354 _____

c. 2 573 _____ **d.** 3 816 _____

e. 4 210 _____ **f.** 3 988 _____

4. Round off each number to the nearest hundred to find an approximate (⌢) total.

a. 313 + 488 ≏ [   ]

b. 275 + 136 ≏ [   ]

c. 841 + 670 ≏ [   ]

5. Round off each price to the nearest dollar and then find the approximate price of all items.

$ 4.08

$ 1.91

$ 2.99

$ 3.99

≏ $ [   ]

Patterns

1. Find the rule for each number pattern.

a. 2 500, 500, 20, 4   Rule _____

b. 2, 4, 8, 16, 32   Rule _____

c. 14, 140, 1 400, 14 000   Rule _____

d. 3, 9, 27, 243   Rule _____

2. Add the missing number or fraction to each pattern.

a. 0.2, 0.4, [   ], 0.8, 1.0, 1.2

b. $\frac{1}{10}, \frac{2}{10}, \frac{3}{10},$ [   ] $, \frac{5}{10}, \frac{6}{10}$

c. $\frac{1}{8}, \frac{1}{4},$ [   ] $, \frac{1}{2}, \frac{5}{8},$ [   ]

d. 3.3, 4.2, 5.1, [   ] , 6.9, 7.8

e. $\frac{1}{6}, \frac{1}{3}, \frac{1}{2}, \frac{2}{3},$ [   ] , 1

3. Fill in the missing numbers in each frame. Follow the rule.

a. Multiply by 5 plus 3.

7	2	4	5	8	3

b. Minus 4, then multiply by 2.

12	17	43	25	13	21

c. Multiply by 3 minus 5.

2	7	9	13	8	6

Angles

Classify each angle as acute, obtuse, right, reflex or straight angle.

a.

_____

b.
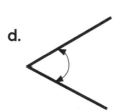

_____

c.

_____

d.

_____

Complete each sentence about types of angles.

a. An angle between 0 degrees and 90 degrees is called a

_____ angle.

b. An angle of 180 degrees is a

_____ angle.

c. An angle between 90 degrees and 180 degrees is an

_____ angle.

d. An angle greater than 180 degrees but less than 360 degrees is a

_____ angle

Label the angle formed in each picture.

a.
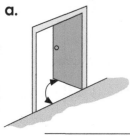

_____

b.
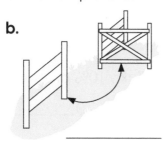

_____

c.
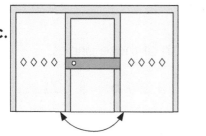

_____

Temperature

1. Show the temperatures on the Celsius scale thermometers.

a. 25ºC   b. 40ºC   c. 65ºC   d. 15ºC

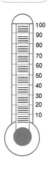 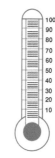 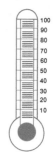 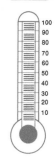

2. Write each temperature in short form. Eg. 25ºC

a. boiling point of water. _____

b. forty-two degrees Celsius. _____

c. sixty-five degrees Celsius. _____

d. freezing point of water. _____

e. normal body temperature. _____

3. Write the temperature showing on each thermometer.

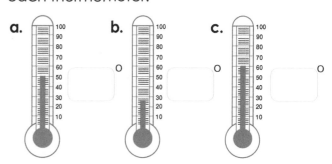

a.   b.   c.

4. Write each temperature in words.

a. 27ºC _____

b. 10ºC _____

c. 0ºC _____

d. 94ºC _____

13

Division

1. Show each number sentence on the number line and calculate remainder.

a. $16 \div 3 =$ ☐   remainder _____

b. $13 \div 4 =$ ☐   remainder _____

c. $17 \div 5 =$ ☐   remainder _____

0 1 2 3 4 5 6 7 8 9 10 11 12 13 14 15 16 17 18 19 20

2. Division can be written formally. Find the quotient for each one.

a. $2\overline{)10}$ **b.** $3\overline{)12}$ **c.** $4\overline{)20}$

d. $6\overline{)24}$ **e.** $5\overline{)35}$ **f.** $7\overline{)49}$

3. Divide the single-digit number into the two-digit number. Write any remainder.

a. $2\overline{)27}^{\ r}$ **b.** $4\overline{)49}^{\ r}$ **c.** $6\overline{)38}^{\ r}$

d. $3\overline{)26}^{\ r}$ **e.** $2\overline{)45}^{\ r}$ **f.** $5\overline{)63}^{\ r}$

4. There are 70 eggs to be put into cartons of 6. How many filled cartons? Remainder?

☐ cartons

☐ left over

14

Fractions

1. Circle the fraction that is **NOT** an equivalent fraction.

a. $\frac{1}{2}$, 0.5 , $\frac{5}{10}$, 50% , 2.5

b. $\frac{1}{4}$, 0.4 , $\frac{2}{8}$, 25% , $\frac{3}{12}$

c. $\frac{1}{5}$, 0.2 , $\frac{2}{10}$, 5% , $\frac{3}{15}$

d. $\frac{3}{6}$, 0.5 , $\frac{1}{3}$ $\frac{6}{12}$, 50%

2. Write the equivalent fraction for each of these.

a. $\frac{1}{3} = \frac{☐}{6}$ **b.** $\frac{1}{2} = \frac{☐}{10}$ **c.** $\frac{1}{2} = \frac{☐}{}$

d. $\frac{4}{12} = \frac{☐}{3}$ **e.** $\frac{2}{3} = \frac{☐}{12}$ **f.** $\frac{3}{5} = \frac{☐}{1}$

g. $\frac{2}{8} = \frac{☐}{4}$ **h.** $\frac{3}{4} = \frac{☐}{8}$ **i.** $\frac{3}{6} = \frac{☐}{}$

3. Write the decimal fraction for each of these

a. $\frac{1}{2} =$ _____   **b.** $\frac{4}{5} =$ _____

c. $\frac{3}{4} =$ _____   **d.** 40% = _____

e. $\frac{1}{5} =$ _____   **f.** $\frac{7}{10} =$ _____

4. Take 10% off each of these prices.

a. $ 70_____   **b.** $ 20_____

c. $ 50_____   **d.** $ 80_____

5. Add 10% to each of these prices.

a. $ 30_____   **b.** $ 60_____

c. $ 40_____   **d.** $ 50_____

2D Shapes

Name each 2D shape.

a.

_____

b.

_____

c.

_____

d.

_____

e.

_____

f.

_____

g.

_____

Name me:

a. I have eight sides and eight angles.

I am _____

b. I have 3 sides, all of different sizes and 3 angles.

I am _____

Draw, then count the diagonals in each shape.

a.

Diagonals

b.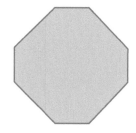

Diagonals

Transformation

1. Enlarge the map by transferring points that cross the grid to the larger grid.

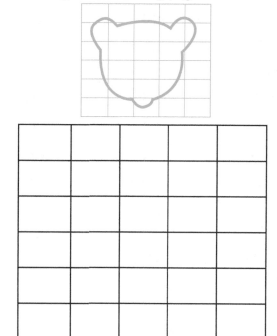

2. Re-draw the cartoon character using the grid.

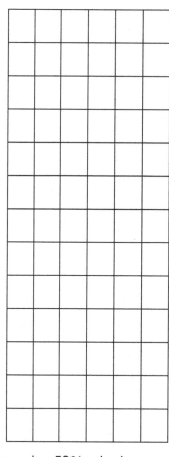

3. If you decrease a shape by 50% what will be its area? Circle your choice.

$$\frac{1}{2} \qquad \frac{1}{4} \qquad \frac{3}{4}$$

15

Tables

1. Complete each set of tables.

a. x2

2x0= _____
2x1= _____
2x2= _____
2x3= _____
2x4= _____
2x5= _____
2x6= _____
2x7= _____
2x8= _____
2x9= _____
2x10=_____

b. x3

3x0= _____
3x1= _____
3x2= _____
3x3= _____
3x4= _____
3x5= _____
3x6= _____
3x7= _____
3x8= _____
3x9= _____
3x10=_____

c. x4

4x0= _____
4x1= _____
4x2= _____
4x3= _____
4x4= _____
4x5= _____
4x6= _____
4x7= _____
4x8= _____
4x9= _____
4x10=_____

d. x5

5x0= _____
5x1= _____
5x2= _____
5x3= _____
5x4= _____
5x5= _____
5x6= _____
5x7= _____
5x8= _____
5x9= _____
5x10=_____

e. x6

6x0= _____
6x1= _____
6x2= _____
6x3= _____
6x4= _____
6x5= _____
6x6= _____
6x7= _____
6x8= _____
6x9= _____
6x10=_____

f. x7

7x0= _____
7x1= _____
7x2= _____
7x3= _____
7x4= _____
7x5= _____
7x6= _____
7x7= _____
7x8= _____
7x9= _____
7x10=_____

g. x8

8x0= _____
8x1= _____
8x2= _____
8x3= _____
8x4= _____
8x5= _____
8x6= _____
8x7= _____
8x8= _____
8x9= _____
8x10=_____

h. x9

9x0= _____
9x1= _____
9x2= _____
9x3= _____
9x4= _____
9x5= _____
9x6= _____
9x7= _____
9x8= _____
9x9= _____
9x10=_____

i. x10

10x0=_____
10x1=_____
10x2=_____
10x3=_____
10x4=_____
10x5=_____
10x6=_____
10x7=_____
10x8=_____
10x9=_____
10x10=_____

Multiplication

1. Complete each number sentence.

a. $14 \times 2 =$ ☐

b. $23 \times 3 =$ ☐

c. $20 \times 4 =$ ☐

d. $31 \times 5 =$ ☐

e. $32 \times 3 =$ ☐

f. $100 \times 7 =$ ☐

g. $300 \times 9 =$ ☐

h. $500 \times 6 =$ ☐

2. Complete each algorithm in its contracted form.

a.
```
  2 324
      2 x
_____

_____
```

b.
```
  1 352
      4 x
_____

_____
```

c.
```
  2 16:
       ⁀
_____

_____
```

d.
```
  1 470
      9 x
_____

_____
```

e.
```
  4 634
      2 x
_____

_____
```

f.
```
  1 23⌐
       7
_____

_____
```

3. A farmer planted 8 rows of grapes. Each row had 145 vines. How many vines in total?

There are_____vines.

4. Complete each money algorithm in its contracted form.

a.
```
$ 21.60
     4 x
_____

_____
```

b.
```
$ 81.45
     5 x
_____

_____
```

c.
```
$ 32.5C
      6
_____

_____
```

5. Multiply the side number by the top number to complete each row.

x	8	10	12	30	20
3					
7					

Nets

me the 3D object made by each net.

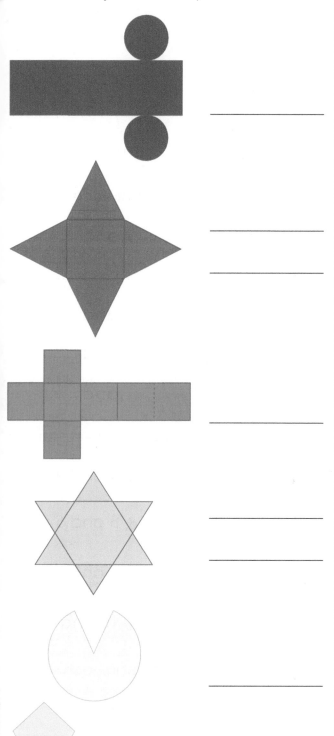

_____

_____
_____

_____

_____
_____

_____

_____
_____

_____
_____

Graphs

Here is a graph showing the number of dresses made in a clothing factory in one week. Use it to answer the questions below.

Day	Key ♀ =10 dresses
Monday	👗👗👗👗👗👗👗👗👗👗
Tuesday	👗👗👗👗👗👗👗👗
Wednesday	👗👗👗👗👗👗👗👗👗
Thursday	👗👗👗👗👗👗👗👗👗
Friday	👗👗👗👗👗👗👗👗
Saturday	👗👗👗👗👗
Sunday	FACTORY CLOSED

1. How many dresses were made on Tuesday?

   _____

2. On which day were
   the most dresses made? _____

3. How many more dresses
   were made on Wednesday
   than on Tuesday? _____

4. On which day were 100 dresses produced?

   _____

5. Suggest which day was only half a work day.

   _____

6. Support your suggestion. _____

   _____

7. On which days were the same number of
   dresses produced?

   _____ _____

8. If there were 3 sections in
   the factory on Thursday
   and each section produced
   the same number, how
   many did one section sew? _____

9. How many dresses were
   made during the week?

17

Problems

1. Ninety-nine marbles are to be shared evenly between three children. How many marbles will each one receive?

 ÷ = each

2. Eighty-three cakes were to be placed on eight plates.

   How many cakes were left over?

3. There are 96 shoes on a shelf, how many pairs are there?

4. A truck travelled 652 kilometres on its first trip, 588 on its second and 1 265 on its third trip. How many kilometres did it travel on the three trips?

   _____ kilometres

5. If the truck needed to refuel every 800 kilometres, how many times was the truck filled with fuel?

6. Mum spent $32.50 on an iron, $23.75 on an ironing board and $9.95 on a cover. How much did she spend?

   $_____change

7. If mum gave the shop keeper a $100 note, what change would she get after buying the Ironing goods?

   $_____change

Multiples and Factors

1. Write the factors for each number.

   a. 18, ___,___, ___, ___, ___,and ___

   b. 20, ___,___, ___, ___, ___,and ___

   c. 12, ___,___, ___, ___, ___,and ___

   d. 10, ___,___, ___, and, ___

2. Write the first 5 multiples of each number.

   a. 3, ___,___, ___, ___,and ___

   b. 2 ___,___, ___, ___,and ___

   c. 5, ___,___, ___, ___,and ___

   d. 4, ___,___, ___, ___,and ___

   e. 6, ___,___, ___, ___,and ___

3. Find the product of each set of numbers.

   a. 4 and 5 =_____   b. 7 and 9 = ____

   c. 9 and 6 =_____   d. 8 and 5 = ___

   e. 7 and 3 =_____   f. 6 and 7 = ____

   g. 5 and 9 =_____   h. 10 and 8 =___

4. Write the missing number in each sentence

   a. [ ] x 8 = 56   b. 7 x [ ] =

   c. 5 x 11 = [ ]   d. 6 x [ ] =

   e. 8 x [ ] = 64   f. [ ] x 5 = 6

5. True (T) or False (F)?

   a. There are 17 threes in 51. _____

   b. 81 is a multiple of 3. _____

   c. 49 is equal to 8 x 7. _____

Mass

Write the mass showing on each bathroom scale.

a.
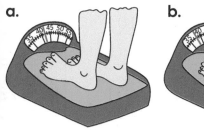
_____ kg

b.
_____ kg

c.
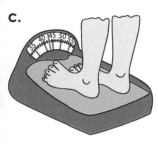
_____ kg

d.
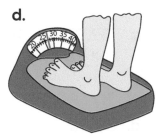
_____ kg

Write the unit of mass you would use to weigh each one using (T) tonne, (kg) kilogram, or (g) gram.

a.

4 _____

b.

895 _____

c.
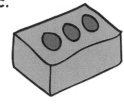
2 _____

d.

500 _____

Write these grams in decimal notation.

a. 835 g _____   b. 1 250 g _____

c. 165 g _____   d. 2 000 g _____

e. 1 500 g _____   f. 2 235 g _____

24 Hour Time

1. Write the clock face afternoon time in 24 hour notation.

a.    b.    c.

d. 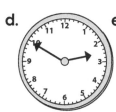   e. 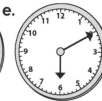   f.

2. Write each time in 24 hours notation.

a. 6 : 30 pm   b. 8 : 45 am

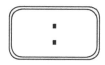

c. 4 : 35 pm   d. 7 : 56 pm

3. Show each time on the clock face.

a. 14 : 25   b. 19 : 35   c. 16 : 40

4. Add 20 minutes to each time.

a. 18 : 56   b. 14 : 45   c. 11 : 50

19

Subtraction

1. Complete each subtraction, with no trading.

a.
TH	H	T	O
7	8	3	6
−2	1	2	5

b.
TH	H	T	O
8	6	9	3
−2	4	4	2

c.
TH	H	T	O
5	6	7	2
−1	2	3	0

d.
TH	H	T	O
7	4	3	8
−2	2	1	7

e.
TH	H	T	O
5	6	7	3
−2	1	4	1

f.
TH	H	T	O
6	6	4	6
−2	5	3	3

2. Complete each subtraction, with trading of ones and tens.

a.
TH	H	T	O
8	3	6	7
−2	2	4	9

b.
TH	H	T	O
7	3	2	8
−1	1	2	7

c.
TH	H	T	O
4	6	3	8
−2	5	0	9

d.
TH	H	T	O
6	8	2	2
−1	4	0	9

e.
TH	H	T	O
7	7	3	6
−2	4	1	8

f.
TH	H	T	O
3	6	7	2
−1	1	1	3

3. Subtract each money algorithm.

a.
H	T	O	T	O
$ 4	2	7 .	5	7
−$ 1	1	6 .	2	9
$			.	

b.
H	T	O	T	O
$ 4	7	2 .	3	2
−$ 1	4	1 .	5	5
$			.	

4. a. Difference between 7 243 and 1 119

b. 400 less than 2 157

Multiplying by 10s and 100

When multiplying by 10 or 100 - add the zeroes.

1. a. 624
        x 10

b. 345
        x 10

c. 8 7
        x

d. 835
        x 100

e. 5 131
        x 100

f. 6 23
        x 10

2. Move the decimal point (one or two plac to the right) when multiplying by 10 or 100

a. 32.72
        x 10

b. 41.53
        x 10

c. 83
        x

d. 83.36
        x 100

e. 45.55
        x 100

f. 17.
        x 1

3. a. Cost of 10 Litres of petrol $ ____
at $2.33 per Litre?

b. Ten kilograms of potatoes $ ____
at $1.75 per kilogram?

c. A batsman averaged 22.2 runs per game of cricket. How many runs did he score in 100 innings?   ____ ru

4. Multiply the top row by the side numbers to complete the table.

x	21.32	42.70	18.62	51.38
10				
100				

5. A can of soft drink holds 375 mL. What is the volume of ten cans of soft drink?

_____

Tessellation

Colour the shapes that can make a tessellating pattern.

a.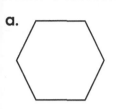
b.
c.

d.
e.
f.

g.
h.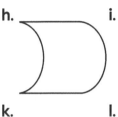
i.

j.
k.
l.

Complete this tessellating pattern. Add colour to the tiles to finish off.

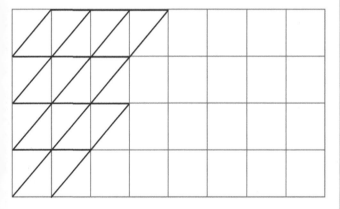

Draw a line to where each shape belongs to make a tile that will tessellate.

a.
b.
c.
d.

e.
f.
g.
h.

Money GST

1. Add GST (Goods & Services Tax) to the price of each item.

a.
b.
c.

$ _____ $ _____ $ _____

d.
e.
f.

$ _____ $ _____ $ _____

2. Some items do not attract GST. Colour those that don't have GST as part of their price.

a.
b.
c.

d.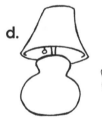
e.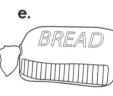
f.

3. Mum bought new furniture for the house. Add the cost then add the GST to find out how much she paid.

Lounge suite . . . . $ 1 250

150 cm television. . . . . $ 875

Two door refrigerator . . .$ 1 380

a. SUBTOTAL _____

b. PLUS GST _____

c. TOTAL PRICE $ _____

21

Addition

1. Add the four-digit numbers with no trading.

a.
TH	H	T	O
3	4	5	3
+2	2	4	4

b.
TH	H	T	O
1	6	7	5
+6	2	2	2

c.
TH	H	T	O
3	7	6	4
+4	1	1	3

2. Add the four-digit numbers but trade tens and ones.

a.
TH	H	T	O
3	6	5	3
+4	2	8	9

b.
TH	H	T	O
4	6	2	7
+1	1	3	8

c.
TH	H	T	O
2	4	6	8
+3	3	7	7

d.
TH	H	T	O
4	5	3	8
+2	1	9	9

e.
TH	H	T	O
1	6	5	6
+6	2	4	8

f.
TH	H	T	O
4	5	3	8
+2	2	8	7

3. Complete each addition square.

a.
18		177	377
86	75	128	
	68	9	328
355	325		994

b.
42	82		169
169		151	390
200	134	268	
	286	464	1 161

4. Complete each number sentence. Check with a calculator.

a. 1 832 + ⬚ + 3 131 = 6 275

b. 295 + 2 300 + ⬚ = 5 382

c. 1 627 + ⬚ + 2 913 = 5 840

d. 4 739 + ⬚ + 1 211 = 6 456

e. 1 824 + 2 156 + ⬚ = 4 562

Equivalent Fractions

1. Write the shaded squares as a fraction.

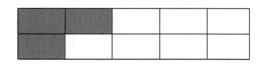

___

2. Add 5/8 and 2/8 = ____

3. Arrange these fractions in rising order.

$\frac{1}{2}$ $\frac{3}{10}$ $\frac{4}{5}$ $\frac{7}{10}$ $\frac{1}{5}$

⬚ ⬚ ⬚ ⬚ ⬚

4. Subtract these fractions. N.B. All have the same denominator.

a. $\frac{7}{8} - \frac{3}{8} =$ ⬚

b. $\frac{3}{5} - \frac{2}{5} =$ ⬚

c. $\frac{3}{4} - \frac{1}{4} =$ ⬚

d. $\frac{7}{12} - \frac{5}{12} =$ ⬚

e. $\frac{5}{8} - \frac{3}{8} =$ ⬚

f. $\frac{2}{3} - \frac{1}{3} =$ ⬚

5. Write the lowest equivalent of each fraction.

a. $\frac{4}{8} =$ ⬚

b. $\frac{3}{12} =$ ⬚

c. $\frac{6}{10} =$ ⬚

d. $\frac{6}{8} =$ ⬚

e. $\frac{2}{10} =$ ⬚

f. $\frac{2}{8} =$ ⬚

6. Write each decimal as a fraction.

a. 0.7= ⬚

b. 0.25= ⬚

c. 0.3= ⬚

d. 0.8= ⬚

e. 0.5= ⬚

f. 0.75= ⬚

7. Change the second fraction to an equivalent fraction then add.

a. $\frac{1}{4} + \frac{1}{2} =$ ⬚

b. $\frac{1}{6} + \frac{2}{3} =$ ⬚

c. $\frac{3}{10} + \frac{1}{2} =$ ⬚

Polygons

Name each polygon.

a.

_____

b.

_____

c.

_____

d.

_____

e.

_____

f.

_____

Draw and then count the diagonals in each polygon.

a.

b.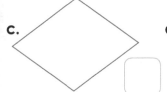

c.

d.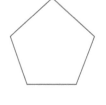

Answer either True (**T**) or False (**F**) to each question about polygons.

a. Polygons have a curved surface.

b. A heptagon has seven sides.

c. A triangle has three diagonals.

d. A circle is not a polygon.

e. An octagon is a polygon.

Timetable

1. Write the 24 hour time in digital form and show it on the clock face.

a. 2318

b. 0640

c. 1210

d. 00.52

2. Use this timetable to answer each question.

Station	Arrive	Depart
Vincent	11:52	11:57
Tully Cross	12:18	12:20
Logonville	12:46	12:50
Sefton	13:09	13:12
Numbleton	13:37	13:40

3. Use this timetable to answer each question.

a. How long does the tram stop at Logonville?

_____

b. How long does it take to travel from Tully Cross to Numbleton?

_____

c. How long does the tram stop at Sefton?

_____

d. If the tram is delayed 6 minutes at Vincent, what time will it arrive at Sefton?

_____

e. If Warnervale is 25 minutes from Numbleton, what time will the tram arrive there?

_____

f. What is the travel time between Vincent and Numbleton?

_____ **23**

Place Value

1. Write the whole number for each expanded number.

 a. 80 000+2 000+900+60+5= _____

 b. 70 000+4 000+200+700+8= _____

 c. 60 000+3 000+800+50+6= _____

 d. 90 000+4 000+70+9= _____

2. Write the words as numerals.

 a. Eighty-seven thousand, six hundred and seventy-eight. _____

 b. Twenty-two thousand, nine hundred and forty-five. _____

 c. Fifty-four thousand, three hundred and ninety-two. _____

 d. Sixty-one thousand, five hundred and seventy-eight. _____

 e. Forty thousand, two hundred and fifty-one. _____

3. Write the number showing on each abacus.

 a. 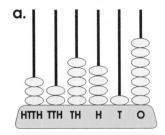   **b.**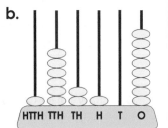

 _____   _____

 c. 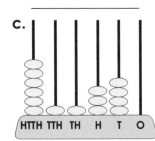   **d.**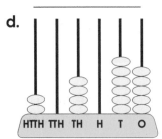

 _____   _____

4. Write the place value for each circled numeral.

 a. 4 ② 3 7 6   **b.** 5 8 ⑤ 7 2

 _____   _____

 c. 6 2 ④ 8 3   **d.** 8 ⑦ 2 5 5

24 _____   _____

Decimals

1. Write each decimal on the number line.

(0.3) (1.2) (0.8) (1.1) (0.5)

(0.9) (0.7) (1.6) (1.9) (0.4)

2. Write the missing middle fraction in each pattern.

 a. 0.4 ☐ 0.6   **b.** 2.2 ☐ 2

 c. 1.5 ☐ 1.9   **d.** 0.6 ☐ 0

 e. 0.8 ☐ 1.2   **f.** 0.5 ☐ 1

3. Fill in the missing decimals in each pattern

 a.

0.1	0.2		0.4		0.6

 b.

1.3	1.5		1.9	2.1	

 c.

1.7	1.6				1.2

4. Add these decimal fractions.

 a. 1.3 + 1.9 = _____   **b.** 2.5 + 0.3 = _____

 c. 0.6 + 2.3 = _____   **d.** 1.9 + 2.2 = _____

 e. 1.4 + 2.9 = _____   **f.** 0.7 + 0.8 = _____

5. Order each group of fractions from smallest to largest.

 a. 0.8, 0.2, 0.9, 0.6, 0.3, 0.5

 _____

 b. 2.4, 1.6, 2.1, 0.7, 1.3, 0.5

 _____

Measuring Angles

Circle the angle less than 60 degrees.

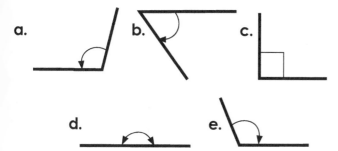

a.   b.   c.

d.   e.

Write in degrees, the angle showing on each protractor.

a.

b.

_____   _____

c.

d.

_____   _____

Name each angle as acute, obtuse, right, reflex or straight.

a.

b.

_____

c.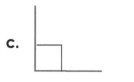

d.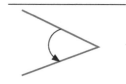

_____   _____

e.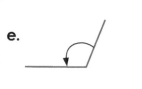

f.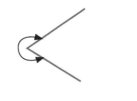

_____   _____

Show each angle on the protractor.

a. 80°

b. 130°

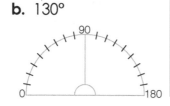

Line Graphs

This line graph shows a bicycle journey for six hours. Use the graph to answer the questions.

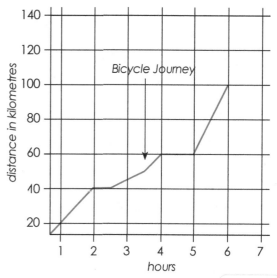

1. How far did the cyclist travel in the first two hours?

2. If the cyclist left home at 7:00 am, what time was the first rest taken?

3. How long was the first rest?

4. How long did it take to travel 60 km?

5. What was the time when the cyclist reached 50 km from home?

6. When was the second rest taken?

7. How long was this rest?

8. How far did the cyclist travel in 6 hours?

9. Extend the graph to show the cyclist travelled 140 km in 7 hours.

10. What was the total rest time taken by the cyclist?

11. With the graph extended to 140 km, at what time will the cyclist arrive there?

25

Rounding Off

1. Round off each number to the nearest 1000.

   a. 76 257 _____   b. 11 962 _____

   c. 81 654 _____   d. 48 161 _____

   e. 27 331 _____   f. 24 681 _____

2. Write the product for each of these using numerals.

   a. Six thousand, four hundred and seventy-three x 100. = _____

   b. Five hundred and ninety-nine x 1 000 = _____

   c. Twenty-two thousand, seven hundred and seventy-six x 10 000 = _____

   d. Ninety-seven thousand and eighty-two x 1 000 = _____

3. Use rounding off strategies to estimate the totals or difference with each of these number sentences. Check actual answers with a calculator.

	Estimate	Actual
a. 5 273 + 4 856 =		
b. 2 983 + 4 152 =		
c. 8 222 + 3 901 =		
d. 4 838 - 1 911=		

4. Estimate these.

   a. 160 eggs, how many dozen?

   b. 450 kilometres driving on 6 Litres of fuel, how many kilometres per Litre?

   c. How many days in 10 ½ weeks?

Square Numbers

1. Match each squared number to its square root.

   a. 2^2 16   b.
            25
   c. 5^2 4   d.
            9
            49
   e. 3^2 36   f.

2. Match each squared number to its square root.

   a. 15^2 144   b.
            64
            81
   c. 8^2 121   d.
            400
   e. 12^2 225   f.

3. Complete the addition and subtraction of each number sentence.

   a. $4^2 + 9^2 =$ ☐   b. $8^2 - 3^2 =$ ☐

   c. $12^2 - 10^2 =$ ☐   d. $7^2 + 2^2 =$ ☐

   e. $5^2 + 5^2 =$ ☐   f. $9^2 - 6^2 =$ ☐

4. Use a calculator to find the square of each number.

   a. $16^2 =$ ☐   b. $21^2 =$ ☐

   c. $13^2 =$ ☐   d. $30^2 =$ ☐

   e. $25^2 =$ ☐   f. $18^2 =$ ☐

5. What number am I?

   I am an odd number less than 30.
   My two digits add to 7.
   I am a square number.

   I am _____

Perimeter

e a ruler to measure the length of each side
the 2D shapes. Add the lengths to find the
rimeter.

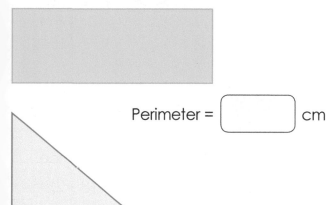

Perimeter = [   ] cm

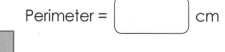

Perimeter = [   ] cm

Perimeter = [   ] cm

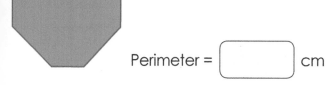

Perimeter = [   ] cm

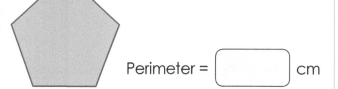

Perimeter = [   ] cm

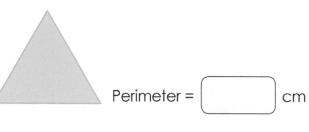

Perimeter = [   ] cm

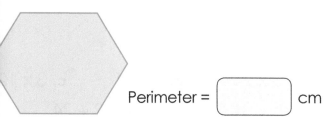

Perimeter = [   ] cm

Location

1. Find streets and landmarks on this road map.
   Use the given co-ordinates to locate and
   write them.

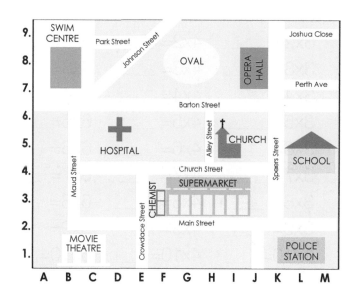

a. B8 _____ b. B6 _____

c. L4 _____ d. J2 _____

e. D5 _____ f. H3 _____

g. J5 _____ h. F3 _____

i. L9 _____ j. L1 _____

k. G7 _____ l. J8 _____

2. As a bike rider take the following route:

   a. Start at J2   b. Travel to E2

   c. Move to E4   d. Turn to H4

   e. Travel to H6   f. Turn to B6

   g. Travel to B2

   h. I have arrived at _____

3. Paris lives on the corner of Alley and Barton
   Streets. Show this position on the map with
   an **X**.

4. Jose lives on the corner of Barton St and
   Speers St. Show this position on the map
   with a circle **O**.

27

Multiplication

Order of Operations

1. Complete the tables.

a. x3

3x0= ____
3x1= ____
3x2= ____
3x3= ____
3x4= ____
3x5= ____
3x6= ____
3x7= ____
3x8= ____
3x9= ____
3x10=____

b. x4

4x0= ____
4x1= ____
4x2= ____
4x3= ____
4x4= ____
4x5= ____
4x6= ____
4x7= ____
4x8= ____
4x9= ____
4x10=____

c. x6

6x0= ____
6x1= ____
6x2= ____
6x3= ____
6x4= ____
6x5= ____
6x6= ____
6x7= ____
6x8= ____
6x9= ____
6x10=____

d. x7

7x0= ____
7x1= ____
7x2= ____
7x3= ____
7x4= ____
7x5= ____
7x6= ____
7x7= ____
7x8= ____
7x9= ____
7x10=____

e. x8

8x0= ____
8x1= ____
8x2= ____
8x3= ____
8x4= ____
8x5= ____
8x6= ____
8x7= ____
8x8= ____
8x9= ____
8x10=____

f. x9

9x0= ____
9x1= ____
9x2= ____
9x3= ____
9x4= ____
9x5= ____
9x6= ____
9x7= ____
9x8= ____
9x9= ____
9x10=____

2. When multiplying a number by 10, 100 or 1 000 just add the zeroes.

a. 62 x
 10
____

b. 78 x
 100
____

c. 98 x
 1 000
_____

c. 833 x
 20
____

d. 4 286 x
 10
_____

e. 143 x
 400
_____

3. Dad spends $50 per week on petrol. How much will he spend in 20 weeks?

28 _____

Remember the order of operations.

> **B** - brackets first.
> **O** - second.
> **D** - division, multiplication, addition or subtraction.

1. Use your knowledge of operations to complete each number sentence.

a. $(4 \times 3) + 9 =$ _____
b. $7 + (8 - 2) =$ ___

c. $24 - (2 + 9) =$ _____
d. $(6 + 3) \times 4 =$ ___

e. $8 + (7 \times 3) =$ _____
f. $(9 + 3) \div 4 =$ ___

g. $(3 + 8) \times 3 =$ _____
h. $4 \times 5 + 8 =$ ___

2. Try these working from left to right.

a. $(4 \times 7) + 5 \div 3 =$ _____

b. $(8 \times 2) - (4 \times 3) =$ _____

c. $36 \div 9 + (3 \times 5) =$ _____

d. $4 \times 2 + (6 + 4) =$ _____

e. $6 \times 3 - (15 \div 3) =$ _____

f. $39 \div 3 + 7 \times 2 =$ _____

3. Use the order of operations for these.

a. $26 - (5 \times 3) + 4 =$ _____

b. $57 + (2 \times 3) - 12 =$ _____

c. $(8 \times 4) - (3 \times 6) + 7 =$ _____

d. $\frac{1}{2}$ of $18 + \frac{1}{4}$ of $16 =$ _____

e. $\frac{1}{4}$ of $100 - \frac{1}{2}$ of $50 =$ _____

4. Circle the statement below that will give you the next number in the series. Write the number.

3, 6, 12, 24, [ ]

a. 3×24
b. 2×24
c. 3×12

d. 24×3
e. $12 + 24$

Capacity

Write the capacity, millilitres (**mL**) or Litres (**L**), of each container.

a.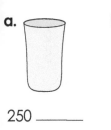

250 _____

b.

220 _____

c.

1 250 _____

d.

25 _____

e.

4 _____

f.

5 _____

Write the capacity of water held in each measuring cylinder.

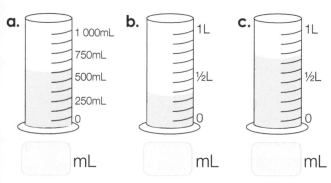

a. 1 000mL / 750mL / 500mL / 250mL / 0

☐ mL

b. 1L / ½L / 0

☐ mL

c. 1L / ½L / 0

☐ mL

List three things found at home that have a capacity of less than one Litre.

_____

_____

_____

Colour the container that would hold the greatest capacity.

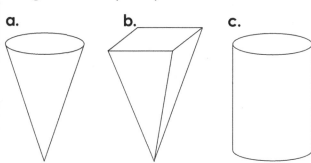

a.   b.   c.

Temperature

1. Show the given temperature on each thermometer.

a. 45°C   b. 62°C   c. 20°C   d. 95°C

2. What is the difference between the hottest and coldest temperatures?

☐ °C

3. Which temperature is closest to the boiling point of water?

☐ °C

4. Which temperature is most likely the closest to today's temperature?

☐ °C

5. Write each temperature in its shortest form.

a. Sixty-two degrees Celsius. _____

b. Freezing temperature of water. _____

c. Boiling point of water. _____

d. Your normal body temperature. _____

e. The temperature it is now. _____

6. Write the temperatures showing on each thermometer.

a.   ☐ °C

b.   ☐ °C

c.   ☐ °C

29

Division with Remainders

1. Write an answer with a remainder for each algorithm.

a. $6\overline{)\,49}^{\quad r}$ **b.** $4\overline{)\,30}^{\quad r}$ **c.** $7\overline{)\,54}^{\quad r}$

d. $8\overline{)\,66}^{\quad r}$ **e.** $5\overline{)\,27}^{\quad r}$ **f.** $9\overline{)\,75}^{\quad r}$

g. $3\overline{)\,52}^{\quad r}$ **h.** $6\overline{)\,39}^{\quad r}$ **i.** $7\overline{)\,59}^{\quad r}$

2. a. How many times can 81 be divided by 3?

b. How many times can 72 be divided by 6?

c. What is the remainder when 105 is divided by 8?

d. What is the remainder when 103 is divided by 3?

3. Write each number sentence in the formal way and then write the quotient and remainder.

a. $167 \div 5 =$ **b.** $247 \div 2 =$ **c.** $528 \div 5 =$

d. $346 \div 6 =$ **e.** $447 \div 8 =$ **f.** $679 \div 6 =$

4. How many groups of 9 in 87? Write the remainder. ☐ r ☐

5. a. Remainder when 37 is divided by 2? ☐

30

b. Remainder when 65 is divided by 7? ☐

Decimal Fractions

1. Write the decimal fraction for each common fraction.

a. $\dfrac{1}{2} =$ ☐   **b.** $\dfrac{1}{4} =$ ☐   **c.** $\dfrac{2}{5} =$ ☐

d. $\dfrac{7}{10} =$ ☐   **e.** $\dfrac{1}{10} =$ ☐   **f.** $\dfrac{3}{5} =$ ☐

g. $\dfrac{3}{4} =$ ☐   **h.** $\dfrac{9}{10} =$ ☐   **i.** $\dfrac{1}{5} =$ ☐

2. Add each group of decimals.

a. $0.2 + 0.5 + 0.2 =$ ☐

b. $0.4 + 0.2 + 0.5 =$ ☐

c. $1.3 + 2.2 + 4.1 =$ ☐

d. $3.2 + 1.4 + 3.6 =$ ☐

e. $4.3 + 3.7 + 2.9 =$ ☐

3. Write the missing fraction in each group as a decimal.

a.

0.2	$\frac{3}{10}$		$\frac{1}{2}$	0.6

b.

	1.1	1.2		$1\frac{2}{5}$	1.5

c.

$\frac{3}{5}$		$\frac{4}{5}$		1	1.1

4. Order each group of decimal fractions in ascending order.

0.7,   1.8,   0.1,   0.9,   0.4,   1.3

a.

3.5,   3.05,   3.15,   3.55,   3.25,   3.2

b.

Mass

Write each mass as a decimal in its shortest form.

a. 4 000 grams _____ **b.** 2 500 grams _____

c. 8 750 grams _____ **d.** 5 250 grams _____

e. $8 \frac{1}{5}$ kg _____ **f.** $6 \frac{1}{2}$ kg _____

g. 1 500 grams _____ **h.** $3 \frac{1}{4}$ kg _____

Write the appropriate unit of mass; grams (**g**), kilograms (**kg**), tonnes (**T**).

a. 90 _____

b. 38 _____

c. 8 _____

d. 20 _____

e. 15 _____

f. 2 _____

Find the mass in grams (g) for each of the following:

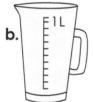

a. 90 millilitres of water

b.

c. 600 mL of water

_____ g _____ g _____ g

If one centi-cube, in these cubes, has a mass of one gram, find the mass of each block.

a.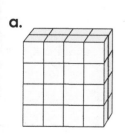

b.

c.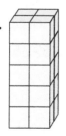

_____ g _____ g _____ g

Ordering Time

1. Order each activity from the earliest to the latest time, using the times provided.

   9am, 1pm, 7am, 7:15am, 11am, 6:30pm, 9:30pm, 3pm, 8am, 4:30pm

   a. Eat lunch at school. _____

   b. Get up in the morning. _____

   c. Do my homework. _____

   d. School begins. _____

   e. Eat dinner with the family. _____

   f. Enjoy my recess break. _____

   g. Leave for school. _____

   h. Go to bed. _____

   i. Have my breakfast. _____

   j. School finishes for the day. _____

2. Write the alphabetical order of events - earliest to latest - beginning with '**b**'

   b. _____

3. Convert each length of time to hours (**hr**), minutes (**min.**) and seconds (**sec.**).

   a. 150 minutes [ ] hr [ ] min ☒ sec

   b. 7 250 seconds [ ] hr [ ] min [ ] sec

   c. 680 second [ ] hr [ ] min [ ] sec

   d. 370 minutes [ ] hr [ ] min ☒ sec

4. Match each event to its appropriate length of time.

   a. a decade — 14 days

   b. a football match — 20 seconds

   c. a fortnight — 80-90 minutes

   d. Able to tie shoe-laces. — 10 years

31

Plus and Minus

1. Round off each number to the nearest thousand.

a. 5 387 _____ **b.** 4 211 _____

c. 3 885 _____ **d.** 6 143 _____

e. 2 972 _____ **f.** 4 848 _____

2. Round off the numbers to estimate a total and then use a calculator to find the actual total.

Estimate   Actual

a. 3 814 + 2 150 =

b. 5 143 + 2 889 =

c. 3 124 + 5 876 =

d. 8 888 + 1 212 =

3. Round off the numbers to estimate the difference and then use a calculator to find the actual difference.

Estimate   Actual

a. 3 163 - 1 212 =

b. 8 708 - 1 690 =

c. 4 867 - 2 799 =

d. 6 259 - 1 360 =

4. Complete the mixed bag of activities by using mental strategies, estimation and a calculator.

a. Sum of 107 + 689 + 800 = _____

b. Add 2 358 + 4 962 = _____

c. Write the sum of 294 and 562 in words.

Pattern Rules

1. Follow each rule to complete a pattern.

a.

Rule x 4 + 1	1	5	21	85	

b.

Rule + 9	36	45	54	63	

c.

Rule ÷ 2	256	128	64	32	

d.

Rule - 7	87	80	73	66	

e.

Rule x 3 + 6	4	18	58	178	

2. Identify the rule for each pattern and then write the last number.

Rul

a. 7, 11, 15, 19, _____

b. 2, 4, 8, 16, _____

c. 243, 81, 27, 9, _____

d. 2, 6, 18, 54, _____

e. 2 785, 278.5, 27.85, _____

3. Complete the decimal pattern. Follow each rule.

a.

Rule + 0.2	0.9	1.1	1.3		

b.

Rule + 1.3	2.6	3.9	5.2		

c.

Rule - 0.5	10.7	10.2	9.7		

d.

Rule -0.3	11.5	11.2	10.9		

e.

Rule +0.9	7.7	8.6	9.5		

4. Multiply or divide each decimal. Move the decimal point left or right.

a. 32.65 ÷ 10 = **b.** 32.65 x 100 = **c.** 24.6 x 1 00

_____   _____   _____

d. 18.75 ÷ 100 = **e.** 1.56 x 1 000 = **f.** 7.29 ÷ 1C

_____   _____   _____

Distance

Add the cardinal and intermediate points to the compass rose.

Use the scaled map to complete the activities.

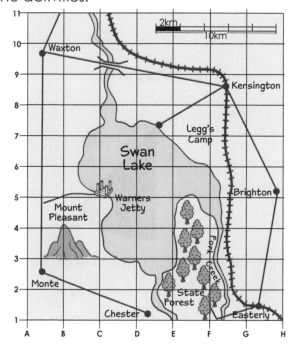

a. In which direction is Monte from Chester? _____

b. Which town is north of Monte? _____

c. What is the distance from Brighton to Kensington? _____

d. Give the co-ordinates for the bridge between Kensington and Waxton. _____

e. In what direction does the railway run to Easterly. _____

f. What is the distance between Monte and Waxton? _____

g. What is the distance from Easterly to Waxton via Kensington? _____

G.S.T.

1. Calculate the price of each item after 10% GST is added.

   a. $95+GST

   b.  $48+GST

   c. $85+GST

   GST = _____   GST = _____   GST = _____

   Total price = $ ____   Total price = $ ____   Total price = $ ____

2. What is meant by G S T ?

   G = _____   S = _____   T = _____

3. Here goods have a GST inclusive price. What part of the price is GST? (÷ by 11)

   a.  $55.00

   b.  $33.00

   GST= _____   GST= _____

   c.  $66.00

   d.  $1 320.00

   GST= _____   GST= _____

4. Some items do not have GST. Wages, rent and some foods are GST free. Identify the items in a budget which have GST added.

			GST	
a.	Apples	$6.50	Yes ☐	No ☐
b.	Petrol	$6.50	Yes ☐	No ☐
c.	Sausages	$6.50	Yes ☐	No ☐
d.	Movie tickets	$6.50	Yes ☐	No ☐
e.	Doctor's visit	$6.50	Yes ☐	No ☐
f.	Groceries	$6.50	Yes ☐	No ☐

5. How much was spent in the above budget? $

6. Do you pay GST on clothes? _____

33

Problems

1. The return adult air fare between Sydney and Los Angeles is $ 3 256.50. How much will it cost for four adults to travel on holidays?

   _____ x _____

2. Tickets to a show cost $9 each. How much money will be raised if 1 482 people attend the show?

   _____ x _____

3. A stamp album page holds eight stamps. If there are 448 stamps to be put in the album, how many pages will be used?

4. If there are 576 children to travel on 8 buses to the Sports Carnival, how many will be on each bus?

5. Which is cheaper to buy? 500 grams of potatoes for $3 or a 2 kilogram bag of potatoes for $10?

   _____

6. How much will Paris need if she buys a pair of running shoes for $89, a tracksuit for $129 and a Polo shirt for $39.50?

   _____

7. If a farmer had 2 755 sheep then sold 2 367, how many sheep would he have left?

8. Pool chlorine is available in 2 kg containers for $10 or 25 kg containers for $100. How much cheaper per kilogram is the bigger container?

Fractions

1. Write each fraction as a decimal.

   a. $\dfrac{27}{100} =$ _____

   b. $\dfrac{9}{10} =$ _____

   c. $\dfrac{4}{5} =$ _____

   d. $\dfrac{80}{100} =$ _____

   e. $\dfrac{1}{2} =$ _____

   f. $\dfrac{1}{4} =$ _____

   g. $\dfrac{44}{100} =$ _____

   h. $\dfrac{1}{5} =$ _____

   i. $\dfrac{3}{10} =$ _____

2. Here is a pie graph showing sports children like to play.

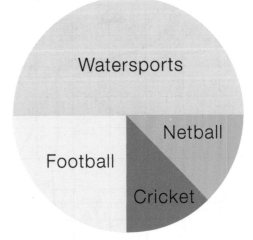

   a. What is the most popular sport?

   _____

   b. What percentage of children like to play water sports? _____

   c. What percentage like football? _____

   d. What two sports are liked equally?

   _____ _____

   e. If 40 children were surveyed, how many like to play football? _____

   f. How many play netball? _____

   g. How many play cricket? _____

3. Circle the fraction that is not an equivalent in each group.

   a. $\dfrac{1}{2}, \dfrac{2}{10}, 0.5$

   b. $\dfrac{3}{4}, 0.5, \dfrac{4}{8}$

   c. $0.3, \dfrac{1}{3}$,

   d. $\dfrac{2}{5}, \dfrac{4}{10}, \dfrac{4}{20}$

   e. $\dfrac{6}{8}, 0.6, \dfrac{3}{4}$

   f. $0.1, \dfrac{1}{5},$

Flip, Slide, Turn

Draw the new shape for each of these.

a. TURN →

b. FLIP →

c. SLIDE →

d. FLIP →

Describe how each shape on the right has moved. Use flip, slide or turn.

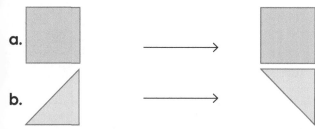

a. →

b. →

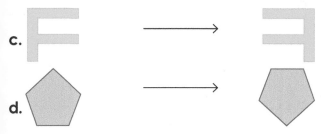

c. →

d. →

How many times does each shape match as it rotates one full turn?

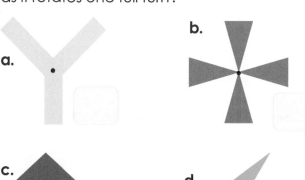

a.

b.

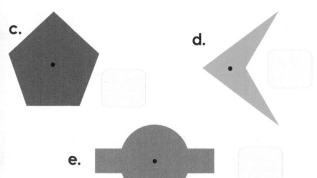

c.

d.

e.

Time

1. Show the 24 hour digital time on the analogue clock.

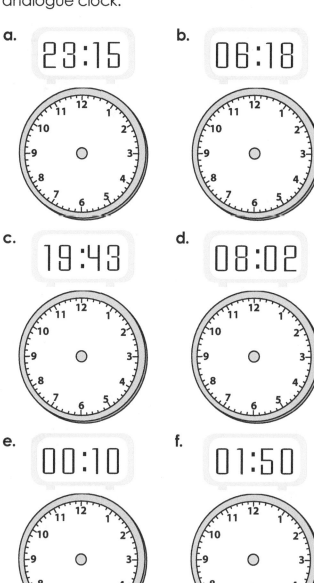

a. 23:15   b. 06:18

c. 19:43   d. 08:02

e. 00:10   f. 01:50

2. Write each time in digital time.

   a. 6:30am   b. 3:30am   c. 1:15am

   d. 10:35pm   e. 8:50pm   f. 5:30pm

3. Write each digital time in am or pm time.

   a. 0614   b. 2210   c. 1040

   _____   _____   _____

   d. 1459   e. 1322   f. 1719

   _____   _____   _____

35

Factors

1. Write the missing factors around the web, for each number.

a.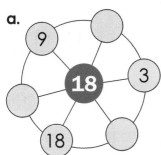

b.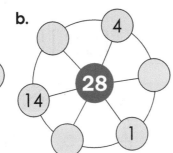

2. Multiply the factors to find the product.

a. 6 x 7 =

b. 4 x 8 =

c. 8 x 3 =

d. 5 x 7 =

e. 9 x 6 =

f. 6 x 4 =

g. 7 x 8 =

h. 3 x 11 =

3. Answer True (**T**) or (**F**) for each statement about factors.

a. 7 is a factor of sixty-three

b. 9 is a factor of eighty-one

c. 6 is a factor of forty-four

d. 5 is a factor of sixty-five

e. 4 is a factor of eighty-six

f. 8 is a factor of seventy-two

4. Find the missing factor for each sentence.

a. 7 x ⬚ = 56

b. 9 x ⬚ = 72

c. ⬚ x 2 = 48

d. 5 x ⬚ = 70

e. 6 x ⬚ = 72

f. ⬚ x 3 = 81

g. 4 x ⬚ = 48

h. ⬚ x 8 = 64

36

Multiplication

1. Use the contracted form to find the produ for each of these.

a.
```
  534
2 x
─────

─────
```

b.
```
  327
3 x
─────

─────
```

c.
```
  126
    4
─────

─────
```

d.
```
  464
2 x
─────

─────
```

e.
```
  137
5 x
─────

─────
```

f.
```
  405
    6
─────

─────
```

2. Write the missing factor on the wheel to match its product.

a.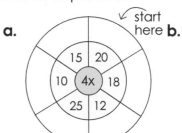

b.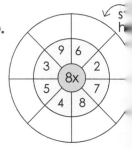

3. a. What is the capacity of 4 cans of soft drink if each can holds 375 mL?

b. One lap around the oval is 750 metres. How far are 7 laps of the oval?

4. Use the contracted form to find the products.

a.
```
  3 214
    3 x
───────

───────
```

b.
```
  6 132
    4 x
───────

───────
```

c.
```
  3 356
      5
───────

───────
```

d.
```
  2 468
    2 x
───────

───────
```

e.
```
  3 172
    6 x
───────

───────
```

f.
```
  4 711
      8
───────

───────
```

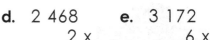

Length

Use the contracted form to find the product for each of these.

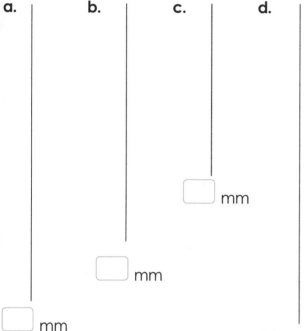

a. _____ mm

b. _____ mm

c. _____ mm

d. _____ mm

Complete the table and then answer the question.

_____ mm = 1cm

100 cm = _____ m

_____ m = 1km

a. 300 mm = _____ cm

b. 4 km = _____ m

c. _____ cm = $\frac{1}{2}$ km

d. _____ cm = 10 m

Use a ruler to measure the perimeter of each 2D shape.

a.  _____ mm

b. 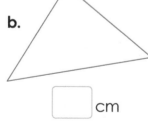 _____ cm

Convert each measurement to metres and centimetres.

a. 1 850 mm = _____ m _____ cm

b. 3 570 mm = _____ m _____ cm

c. 10 380 mm = _____ m _____ cm

d. 4 700 mm = _____ m _____ cm

Chance

1. Match the chance fractions to a possible outcome.

a. Roll a die and turn up 3

b. Toss a coin and turn up a tail.

c. Toss two coins and turn up two heads.

d. Land a one on a pentagonal spinner.

$\frac{1}{2}$

$\frac{1}{4}$

$\frac{1}{5}$

$\frac{1}{6}$

$\frac{1}{8}$

$\frac{1}{3}$

e. Win a four horse race.

f. Land on red.

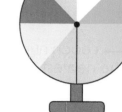

2. A counter with one side red and the other side blue is tossed into the air three times. Colour the counters to show the possible outcomes.

a.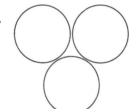

b.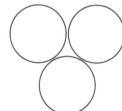

c.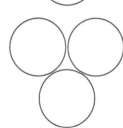

d.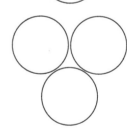

3. If you have a pack of 52 playing cards of which 26 are red and 26 black:

a. What chance do you have of selecting a black card? _____

b. There are 6 red picture cards and 6 black picture cards. What is the chance of picking a red picture card? _____

c. There are four suits in the pack. What is the chance of picking a diamond card? _____

d. If the heart cards are removed, what is the chance of picking a red card? _____

37

Rounding Off

1. Round off each sum of money to the nearest 5 cents.

   a. 87 cents   **b.** $1.08   **c.** $3.43

   d. $7.02   **e.** $5.89   **f.** $6.44

2. Join each number, rounded off to the nearest 100, on the number line.

   (674)   (238)   (519)   (189)

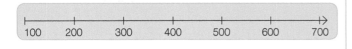

100 200 300 400 500 600 700

   (327)   (625)   (448)   (692)

3. Round off each number to the nearest 1 000.

   a. 8 361 _____   **b.** 4 833 _____

   c. 5 469 _____   **d.** 3 782 _____

   e. 4 993 _____   **f.** 2 438 _____

4. Round off each sum of money to the nearest dollar.

   a. $7.37   **b.** $8.65   **c.** $3.21

   d. $10.89   **e.** $117.30   **f.** $868.51

5. Find the approximate totals for each of these additions.

   a. 898 + 301 ≏ _____   **b.** 607 + 391 ≏ _____

   c. 411 + 592 ≏ _____   **d.** 506 + 295 ≏ _____

Division with Remainders

1. Use the contracted form to complete each division. Don't forget remainders!

   a. 5) 277 r   **b.** 3) 826 r   **c.** 4) 38 r

   d. 2) 713 r   **e.** 6) 255 r   **f.** 7) 85 r

2. Use the contracted form to divide numbers where a zero is part of the dividend.

   a. 5) 516 r   **b.** 6) 627 r   **c.** 4) 43 r

   d. 7) 765 r   **e.** 6) 656 r   **f.** 8) 84 r

3. Jon, Omar, Darcy and Xavier won a prize $685. It was shared equally in whole dollars. Any left over was put into the 'poor box'. How much did each boy get and how much was put into the 'poor box'?

   a. Each boy received _____

   b. The poor box received _____

4. Find the missing number in each division algorithm.

   a. ☐) 724 = 241 r1   **b.** 5) 68☐ = 137 r2

   c. 4) 6☐7 = 164 r1   **d.** 6) 704 = 1☐7 r2

   e. 3) 841 = 28☐ r1   **f.** 2) 735 = ☐67 r1

Area

Write the most appropriate unit of area for each shape. (m², ha or km²).

a.

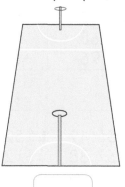

b.

c.

f.

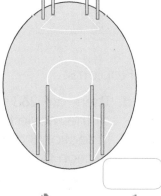

e.

f.

Complete each statement to make it true.

a. _____ha=km²   **b.** 3ha= _____ m²

c. 8 000m²=_____ ha **d.** 900ha=_____ km²

e. 500ha=_____km² **f.** 10 000m²=_____ha

Use the scale 1cm = 20m to find the perimeter and area of each shape.

a.

Perimeter _____

Area _____

b.

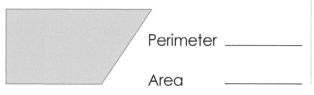

Perimeter _____

Area _____

Line Graphs

Here is a line graph showing the average daily temperatures for each month of the year. Use the graph to help answer the questions.

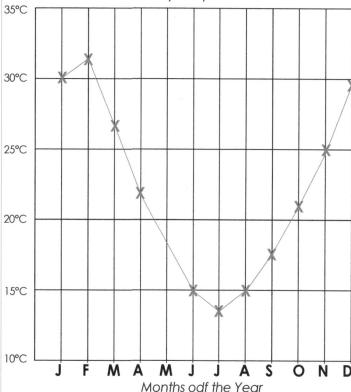

1. What is the average temperature for January? _____

2. Which two months have about the same average temperature?

   _____   _____

3. Which month averaged 27°C?

   _____

4. How many months average 25°C or below? _____

5. Which is the hottest month? _____

6. Which month is the coldest?_____

7. Does it get hotter in the two months that follow December? _____

8. Which months range between 25°C and 30°C? _____

9. Why are the temperatures low in June, July and August?

   _____

39

Using a Calculator

1. Write the decimal for each fraction. Use a calculator and divide the numerator into the denominator.

a. $\dfrac{1}{2} =$ 　　**b.** $\dfrac{1}{4} =$ 　　**c.** $\dfrac{1}{5} =$

d. $\dfrac{2}{3} =$ 　　**e.** $\dfrac{3}{4} =$ 　　**f.** $\dfrac{3}{10} =$

g. $\dfrac{3}{5} =$ 　　**h.** $\dfrac{3}{8} =$ 　　**i.** $\dfrac{4}{5} =$

2. Use a calculator to convert each fraction to a percentage. Divide the numerator by the denominator then press %

a. $\dfrac{4}{5} =$ ____% 　**b.** $\dfrac{7}{10} =$ ____% 　**c.** $\dfrac{1}{4} =$ ____%

d. $\dfrac{7}{8} =$ ____% 　**e.** $\dfrac{2}{5} =$ ____% 　**f.** $\dfrac{9}{10} =$ ____%

g. $\dfrac{1}{5} =$ ____% 　**h.** $\dfrac{5}{8} =$ ____% 　**i.** $\dfrac{1}{10} =$ ____%

3. Use the M+ button to add each calculation and the MR to total the separate operations.

a. 6 x 3　M+ 　　**b.** 8 x 5　M+ 　　**c.** 4 x 3　M+
　+5 x 4　M+ 　　　+7 x 3　M+ 　　　+6 x 5　M+
　+2 x 6　M+ 　　　+6 x 6　M+ 　　　+4 x 9　M+

MR _____ 　　　MR _____ 　　　MR _____

4. Do each horizontal addition using M+ and MR

a. 5 x 4 + 7 x 3 + 6 x 5 = 　_____

b. 3 x 9 + 5 x 8 + 7 x 8 = 　_____

c. 8 x 9 + 5 x 7 + 2 x 9 = 　_____

d. 7 x 7 + 6 x 9 + 8 x 9 = 　_____

5. Use a calculator to find the next 2 numbers in each pattern.

x4	7	28	112		
+26	2	28	54		
÷2	128	64	32		

40

Addition

1. Find the total of each money sum.

a. $27.64
　　$18.37
　+$15.89

　$ _____

b. $48.32
　　$59.68
　+$38.95

　$ _____

c. $72.
　　$87.
　+$69.

　$ _____

d. $176.52
　　$239.75
　+$188.96

　$ _____

e. $385.49
　　$267.38
　+$444.78

　$ _____

f. $523.
　　$127.8
　+$159.2

　$ _____

2. Problems:

a. There are 268 seats in section **A** at the movie theatre, 76 seats in section **B** and 786 seats in section **C**. How many seats in the three sections? 　_____

　　　　Total seats _____

b. Year 5 had three cake stalls. The takings at each stall were $58.95, $126.80 and $79.35. How much was taken altogether? 　_____

Total for the stalls $ _____

3. Find the missing numbers in each addition

a.
　6 378
　4 ☐93
+2 646
13 3☐7

b.
　4 538
　6 ☐17
+5 429
16 88☐

c.
　2 47
　1 76
+3 ☐8
　7 8

d.
　8 35☐
　7 223
+1 469
17 ☐50

e.
　6 6☐6
　7 253
+ ☐465
18 364

f.
　2 9 6
　1 5
+2 ☐8
　7 22

Volume

Count the one centimetre cubes in each model to find its volume.

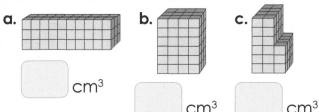

a. ☐ cm³

b. ☐ cm³ c. ☐ cm³

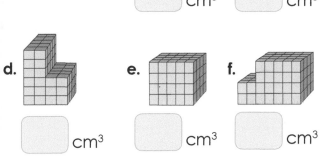

d. ☐ cm³ e. ☐ cm³ f. ☐ cm³

Use the formula, length x height x depth, (**L x H x D**) to find the volume of each model.

a.

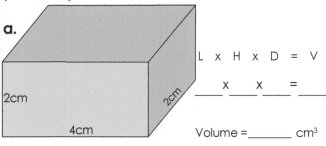

2cm 2cm 4cm

L x H x D = V

___ x ___ x ___ = ___

Volume = _____ cm³

b.

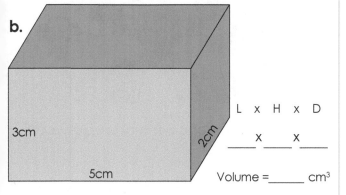

3cm 2cm 5cm

L x H x D

___ x ___ x ___

Volume = _____ cm³

Write the unit of volume for each measurement. (m³ or cm³ or mm³)

a. 8 cubic metres   b. 12 cubic centimetres

_____   _____

c. 240 cubic millimetres

_____

d. 27 cubic metres e. 164 cubic centimetres

_____   _____

A unit of centicubes has a volume of 8 cm³. How many centicubes in a unit with a volume of 56 cm³?

Graphs and Charts

1. This bar graph shows how 54 Year 5 children travel to school. Use a ruler to measure the number of children on the graph who fit into each category and then answer each question,

Scale 5mm = 3 children

walk	train	bus	car

a. How many children travel by car? _____

b. How many travel by bus? _____

c. How many more children walk than come by train? _____

d. How many children walk? _____

e. How many come to school using wheels? _____

2. Here is a pie chart showing how 50 children choose their sport.

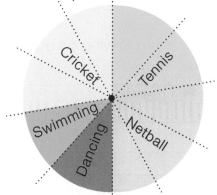

Scale: 1 piece of pie = 5 children

a. How many children play cricket? _____

b. How many play tennis? _____

c. How many choose swimming? _____

d. Is dancing a popular choice? _____

e. What were the two sports where 15 children participate?

_____   _____

f. How many more children play cricket than tennis? _____

g. How many children play ball sports? _____

Ordering Fractions

1. Write each fraction as a decimal and as a percentage.

   a. $\frac{47}{100}$ = ⬚ . ⬚ = ⬚ %   b. $\frac{4}{5}$ = ⬚ . ⬚ = ⬚ %

   c. $\frac{7}{10}$ = ⬚ . ⬚ = ⬚ %   d. $\frac{3}{4}$ = ⬚ . ⬚ = ⬚ %

   e. $\frac{1}{4}$ = ⬚ . ⬚ = ⬚ %   f. $\frac{79}{100}$ = ⬚ . ⬚ = ⬚ %

2. Arrange the decimals in ascending order.

   a. 0.85, 0.17, 0.36, 0.92, 0.09

   _____

   b. 1.02, 0.47, 1.46, 0.84, 0.05

   _____

   c. 2.98, 0.93, 1.46, 0.89, 1.24

   _____

3. Write the fraction showing on each place value card.

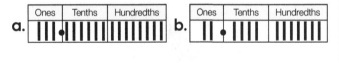

   a. _____   b. _____

   c. _____   d. _____

4. Order each fraction on the place value cards in descending order.

   _____

5. Write as a decimal the fraction showing on each diagram.

 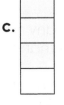 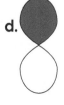

   a. ____   b. ____   c. ____   d. ____

Subtraction

1. Using the contracted form, find the difference between the numbers.

   a.   6 425
      −1 113
      _____

   b.   8 679
      −4 257
      _____

   c.   3 9
      −1 7⋮
      _____

   d.   8 751
      −2 437
      _____

   e.   9 684
      −2 369
      _____

   f.   5 6⋮
      −1 48
      _____

2. Problems:

   a. The local High School has 1 248 students. 289 Year 7 students went on an excursion. How many students were left at school?

      − _____
      _____

   b. A cattle station has 5 375 head of cattle. 2 468 are sent to another farm for better feed. How many cattle were left behind?

      − _____
      _____

3. Find the difference in money between each one.

   a. $325.52
      −$113.20
      _____

   b. $ 476.25
      −$ 322.20
      _____

   c. $867.⋮
      −$246.⋮
      _____

   d. $736.45
      −$137.18
      _____

   e. $563.20
      −$144.17
      _____

   f. $617.⋮
      −$205.⋮
      _____

4. Subtract to find the missing numbers.

   a.   3 ⬚ 16
      − 1 433
      _____
      2 2 ⬚ 3

   b.   4 8 ⬚ 6
      − 1 468
      _____
      3 ⬚ 58

   c.   3 47
      − 1 25
      _____
      2 2

Capacity

Write the unit of capacity for each container.
Use either millilitres (**mL**) or Litres (**L**)

a.

b.

c.

200 _____   375 _____   1 _____

d.

e.

f.

200 _____   150 _____   5 000 _____

If one cup holds 250 millilitres, how many cups will each of the following hold?

a. 500mL = _____ cups   **b.** 750mL = _____ cups

c. 1.5L = _____ cups   **d.** 910L = _____ cups

e. $4\frac{1}{2}$ L = _____ cups   **f.** 2 250mL = _____ cups

Add the capacities together.
Write each total as Litres and millilitres.

a. 3L 240mL + 6L 585mL + 5L 750mL =

[____] L [____] mL

b. 950mL + 3L 250mL + 3L 275mL =

[____] L [____] mL

c. 2L 325mL + 4L 580mL + 5L 750mL =

[____] L [____] mL

How many millilitres in each measurement?

a. 1.5L = _____ mL   **b.** 5.54L = _____ mL

c. 2.35L = _____ mL   **d.** 6.250L = _____ mL

e. $3\frac{3}{4}$ L = _____ mL   **f.** $4\frac{1}{2}$ L = _____ mL

Chance

Roll a die to achieve a specific number.

Roll 3	Tally	Total

Roll 6	Tally	Total

Roll 1	Tally	Total

Roll 5	Tally	Total

Roll 4	Tally	Total

Roll 2	Tally	Total

1. Count the number of times you rolled the die before the specific number turned up.

2. Which number was the quickest to turn up?

3. Which number took the most throws before turning up?

4. Did any number turn up first throw? _____

5. What fractional chance do you have of turning up a 6 first throw? _____

6. Write the fraction to express the chance of landing on the given number.

a.
1 3
2 4

4 = —

b.
5 9
6 8
7

8 = —

c.
9 2
5   6
8   4
3 7

2 = —

d.
2 1 10
3   9
4   8
5 6 7

5 = —

e.
3 9
6

3 = —

f.
2 16
4   14
6   12
8 10

12 = —

7. Answer either, **possible** OR **impossible**, for each statement.

a. Mum will win lotto tonight _____

b. I can roll a seven on a die. _____

c. Toss two coins and both will land on heads.   _____ **43**

Equivalent Factors

1. Colour the square in each that is not an equivalent fraction.

a.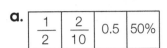

| $\frac{1}{2}$ | $\frac{2}{10}$ | 0.5 | 50% |

b.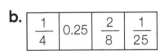

| $\frac{1}{4}$ | 0.25 | $\frac{2}{8}$ | $\frac{1}{25}$ |

c.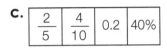

| $\frac{2}{5}$ | $\frac{4}{10}$ | 0.2 | 40% |

d.

| 60% | 6.0 | $\frac{3}{5}$ | $\frac{6}{10}$ |

e.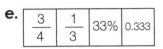

| $\frac{3}{4}$ | $\frac{1}{3}$ | 33% | 0.333 |

f.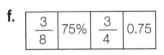

| $\frac{3}{8}$ | 75% | $\frac{3}{4}$ | 0.75 |

2. Match the equivalent fraction to the correct diagram.

a.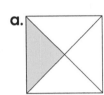

$\frac{1}{3}$

0.5

b.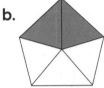

c.

$\frac{4}{10}$

25%

d.

e.

$\frac{4}{5}$

75%

f.

3. Write the fraction shaded on each hundred grid as a percentage, decimal and fraction in hundreds.

a.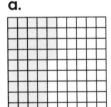

_____ %

0. _____

$\overline{}$
100

b.

_____ %

0. _____

$\overline{}$
100

c.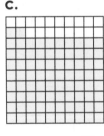

_____ %

0. _____

$\overline{}$
100

4. Write an equivalent fraction for each one.

a. $\frac{1}{2} = \frac{\square}{4}$ **b.** $\frac{4}{5} = \frac{\square}{10}$ **c.** $0.6 = \frac{\square}{5}$

d. $\frac{3}{4} = \frac{\square}{8}$ **e.** $\frac{1}{2} = \frac{\square}{10}$ **f.** $\frac{3}{4} = \frac{\square}{100}$

44

Decimal Fractions

1. Join each decimal fraction to its position on the number line.

(0.4) (1.6) (2.5) (0.25) (2.8) (1.2

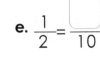

2. Arrange each group of fractions in rising order.

a. 0.35, 0.75, 0.21, 0.15, 0.62, 0.53

_____

b. 1.47, 2.68, 0.75, 3.62, 1.33, 2.07

_____

c. 0.55, 0.72, 0.16, 1.6, 1.09, 0.53

_____

3. Write the middle number between each p

a. 2.7_____ 2.9   **b.** 1.62 _____ 1.6

c. 2.25_____2.75   **d.** 1.2 _____ 1.

e. 0.04_____0.08   **f.** 0.3 _____ 0.

4. Identify the place value of each circled number. (tens, ones, tenths, hundredths)

a. 3 2 . 4 ③_____

b. 5 ③ . 6 7_____

c. 3 9 . ⑤ 5_____

d. ⑥ 4 . 3 9_____

5. Write the sum of each as decimal fraction

a. 42.46
+131.75

_____

b. 29.49
+33.68

_____

c. 243.9
+ 72.0

_____

Mass

Match each object to its correct mass.

10g

2T

5kg

2kg

300kg

275g

3kg

45kg

Write each mass in its shortest form.

a. 3 000g _____ b. 4 500g _____

c. 10 200g _____ d. 6 500g _____

e. 8kg 500g _____ f. 10kg 250g _____

Find the mass of each model if 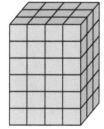 has a mass of 2 grams.

a.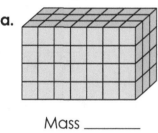

Mass _____

b.

Mass _____

d.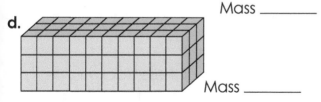

Mass _____

Problems:

a. A coal train has 72 carriages, each carrying 30 tonnes of coal. How much coal does the train carry?

_____ x

_____

b. Jelly Beans are priced at $12 per kilogram. How much will 300 grams cost?

_____ x

_____

Time

1. Write the digital time for each pm time.

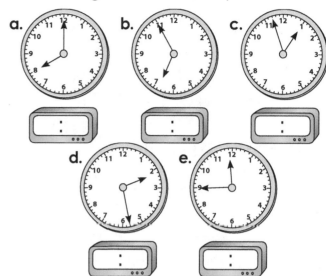

2. Write each time in words.

a. 7:30 _____

b. 14:25 _____

c. 18:15 _____

d. 23:45 _____

e. 00:01 _____

3. Write a personal time-line for each event.

a. The year your mother was born. _____

b. The year you were aged 5. _____

c. The year the family bought a car. _____

d. The year it is now. _____

4. Find the year each event happened.

a. Arthur Phillip arrived in Sydney. _____

b. Australia became a Federation. _____

c. World War 1 began. _____

d. The ANZAC landing at Gallipoli. _____

45

Money

1. Colour the items that attract a GST.

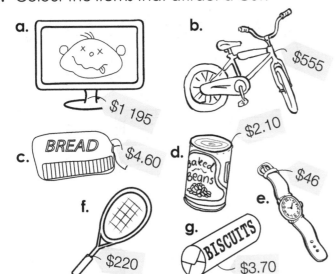

a. $1 195
b. $555
c. BREAD $4.60
d. baked Beans $2.10
e. $46
f. $220
g. BISCUITS $3.70

2. Look at each discount and find the new price for the item.

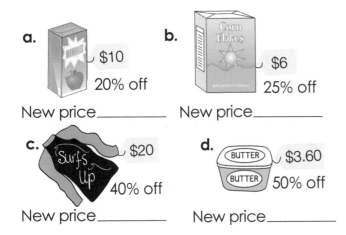

a. $10   20% off
New price_____

b. Corn Flakes $6   25% off
New price_____

c. Surf's Up $20   40% off
New price_____

d. BUTTER $3.60   50% off
New price_____

3. Find the cost and then the change from $100 for each group of items.

a. 2 polo shirts @ $39.50 each.

Cost $_____ Change $_____

b. A toaster @ $42.50 and a lamp @ $38.

Cost $_____ Change $_____

c. School shoes @ $49.95 and shorts @ $27.

Cost $_____ Change $_____

4. Remember to know cost of GST you divide by 11. What is the GST on each price?

a. $22_____ b. $88_____ c. $55_____

46 d. $209_____ e. $143_____ f. $715_____

Fractions

1. Change the denominator to make an equivalent, common fraction.

a. $\dfrac{2}{5} = \dfrac{4}{\square}$

b. $\dfrac{3}{4} = \dfrac{6}{\square}$

c. $\dfrac{1}{2} = \dfrac{5}{\square}$

d. $\dfrac{1}{4} = \dfrac{3}{\square}$

e. $\dfrac{1}{3} = \dfrac{2}{\square}$

f. $\dfrac{4}{5} = \dfrac{8}{\square}$

2. Change each fraction to the lowest form

a. $\dfrac{3}{9} = —$

b. $\dfrac{6}{10} = —$

c. $\dfrac{6}{8} = —$

d. $\dfrac{10}{20} = —$

e. $\dfrac{14}{20} = —$

f. $\dfrac{4}{16} = —$

3. Use your knowledge of fraction to add each one.

Remember: To add or subtract fractions each fraction needs to be equivalent first.

One is done for you.

$\dfrac{1}{4} + \dfrac{1}{2} =$

a. $\dfrac{1}{4} + \dfrac{3}{8} =$

b. $\dfrac{1}{5} + \dfrac{3}{10} =$

$\dfrac{1}{4} + \dfrac{2}{4} = \dfrac{3}{4}$

$\dfrac{}{8} + \dfrac{}{8} = —$

$\dfrac{}{10} + \dfrac{}{10} = —$

c. $\dfrac{1}{8} + \dfrac{1}{4} =$

d. $\dfrac{1}{6} + \dfrac{2}{3} =$

e. $\dfrac{2}{5} + \dfrac{1}{2} =$

$\dfrac{}{} + \dfrac{}{} = —$

$\dfrac{}{} + \dfrac{}{} = —$

$\dfrac{}{} + \dfrac{}{} = —$

4. Subtract each of these fractions.

a. $\dfrac{9}{10} - \dfrac{1}{2} =$

b. $\dfrac{7}{8} - \dfrac{1}{4} =$

c. $\dfrac{3}{4} - \dfrac{1}{2} =$

$\dfrac{9}{10} - \dfrac{5}{10} = \dfrac{4}{10}$

$\dfrac{}{8} + \dfrac{}{8} = —$

$\dfrac{}{10} + \dfrac{}{10} = —$

d. $\dfrac{7}{8} - \dfrac{1}{2} =$

c. $\dfrac{5}{6} - \dfrac{2}{3} =$

f. $\dfrac{1}{2} - \dfrac{1}{5} =$

$\dfrac{}{} + \dfrac{}{} = —$

$\dfrac{}{} + \dfrac{}{} = —$

$\dfrac{}{} + \dfrac{}{} = —$

Temperature

Colour the temperature to the correct level on each Celsius scaled thermometer.

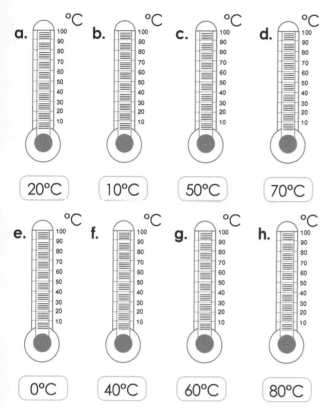

a. 20°C   b. 10°C   c. 50°C   d. 70°C

e. 0°C   f. 40°C   g. 60°C   h. 80°C

Write each Celsius temperature in numerals.

a. Twenty seven degrees   **b.** Zero degrees

_____°C   _____°C

c. One hundred degrees   **d.** Twenty degrees

_____°C   _____°C

Match each season to its average temperature.

Autumn	30°C	Spring
	20°C	
	18°C	
Summer	12°C	Winter

Write the approximate temperature that could occur to the times of the year.

a. Christmas Day _____

b. 1st May (May Day) _____

c. The Queen's Birthday weekend _____

d. The Royal Easter Show _____

e. New Years Day _____

f. The begining of Term 4 _____

Data Combinations

1. Here is a menu at a local restaurant. Fill out the possible combinations for a three course meal beginning with soup.

Menu For Kids

Entrees	Soup	$5
	Salad	$6
Mains	Chicken Nuggets	$6
	Fish and Chips	$7
	Hamburger	$8
Desserts	Ice cream	$5
	Chocolate cake	$4

Soup

a.

b.

2. How many combinations are there with soup? ☐

3. If the salad selections were set out also, How many combinations could be selected? ☐

4. Write the three course combination that would be the cheapest.

_____ _____ _____

5. How much would that selection cost? _____

6. Write the three course combination that would be the most expensive.

_____ _____ _____

7. Here is a double ice-cream cone and the choice of 3 flavours. Write the possible combinations.

_____

Strawberry   _____

_____

Chocolate   _____

_____

Vanilla   _____

47

Order of Operations

Fractions and Patterns

1. Complete each number sentence. Do the brackets first.

a. $6 \times (4 + 6) =$ _____   b. $(8 - 2) \times 23 =$ _____

c. $8 \times (2 + 9) =$ _____   d. $(3 + 2) \times 9 =$ _____

e. $(3 \times 8) \div 6 =$ _____   f. $(7 \times 3) + 9 =$ _____

g. $(6 \div 2) \times 5 =$ _____   h. $(12 \div 4) + 2 =$ _____

2. Working from left to right, find the answer for these.

a. $6 \times (8 + 3) - (7 - 2) \times 5 =$

b. $51 \div 3 - (5 \times 2) + 6 =$

c. $(15 \times 4) + (27 \div 9) - 5 =$

d. $(24 - 8) \times 3 + (33 \div 11) =$

3. In a number sentence the 'of' means multiplying. The 'of' operation is done last.

a. $(\frac{1}{2}$ of $6) + 3 =$ b. $(\frac{1}{3}$ of $18) + 3 =$

c. $(\frac{1}{4}$ of $20) - 2 =$ d. $(\frac{1}{8}$ of $32) - 2 =$

e. $(\frac{3}{4}$ of $16) + 9 =$ f. $(\frac{1}{2}$ of $2) + 8 =$

4. Try each money operation.

a. $\frac{1}{3}$ of $\$ 30 =$ b. $\frac{1}{2}$ of $\$ 90 =$

c. $\frac{1}{5}$ of $\$ 75 =$ d. $\frac{1}{6}$ of $\$ 42 =$

e. $\frac{3}{4}$ of $\$ 80 =$ f. $\frac{7}{10}$ of $\$ 50 =$

5. Complete each number sentence. Follow the order of operations.

a. $18 \div 2 \times (3 + 4) =$

b. $\frac{1}{5}$ of $20 \times 7 =$

c. $(22 - 8) \times \frac{1}{2}$ of $6 =$

d. $\frac{1}{8}$ of $32 \times (36 + 4) =$

---

1. Write the decimal fraction showing on each place value card.

a.
Ones	Tenths	Hundredths
III	II	IIIIIII

b.
Ones	Tenths	Hundred
III	III	IIII

_____

_____

c.
Ones	Tenths	Hundredths
IIII	IIII	II

d.
Ones	Tenths	Hundred
II		IIII

_____

_____

2. Write the missing numbers in each pattern.

a.
| $\frac{1}{4}$ | $\frac{1}{2}$ | $\frac{3}{4}$ | 1 | | |

b.
| 0.3 | 0.5 | 0.7 | 0.9 | | |

c.
| 3.25 | 3.5 | | 4 | | 4.5 |

d.
| 1.08 | 1.06 | | 1.02 | | 0.9 |

3. Write the fraction for each shape.

a.
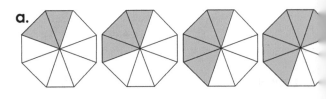

_____   _____   _____   _____

b.
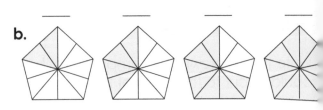

_____   _____   _____   _____

4. Match the fractions and decimals to the number line.

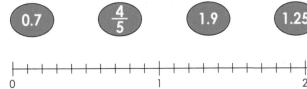

0.7 $\frac{4}{5}$ 1.9   1.25

$\frac{1}{2}$ 2.2   0.3 $1\frac{3}{5}$

Faces and Nets

Match each 3D object to its net.

a.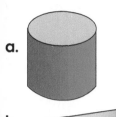

e.

f.

b.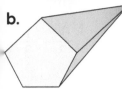

c.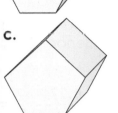

g.

d.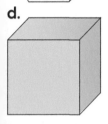

h.

Draw the shape on the opposite side of the cube.

a.   b.   c.   d.

opposite   opposite   opposite   opposite

Name the 3D solid each net would make.

a.   b.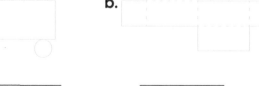

_____   _____

c.    d.

_____   _____

Location

1. Identify the position of objects on the grid. Draw the shape alongside the co-ordinates.

	A	B	C	D	E	F	G	H	I	J	
		★									1
				♥			○		⊕		2
	Ω					A		✚			3
			≣							▼	4
			●		✓			🍦			5
	▨						‖‖				6
		◇						△		Σ	7
			✿								8

a. G6 _____   b. A3 _____   c. B1 _____

d. G2 _____   e. H7 _____   f. H3 _____

g. D8 _____   h. C5 _____   i. I2 _____

j. H5 _____   k. B4 _____   l. J7 _____

m. F3 _____   n. A6 _____   o. D2 _____

p. B7 _____   q. J4 _____   r. E5 _____

2. Write the cardinal points on each rose.

a. S   b.    c. E

W

3. Write the co-ordinates for each letter.

	A	B	C	D	E	F	G	H	I	J
1		g				i				n
2			a				o		d	
3	k				f			h		
4				j			b			
5		c								e
6			l			m				

a. _____   b. _____   c. _____   d. _____

e. _____   f. _____   g. _____   h. _____

i. _____   j. _____   k. _____   l. _____

m. _____   n. _____   o. _____

Decimals and Percentage

+ and - Fractions

1. Write the percentages as fractions.

a. 50% = ⬭ **b.** 40% = ⬭ **c.** 75% = ⬭

d. 90% = ⬭ **e.** 10% = ⬭ **f.** 8% = ⬭

2. Write each number of shaded squares as a decimal fraction.

a. 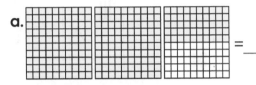 = _____

b. 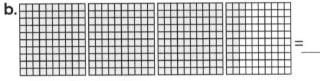 = ___

c. 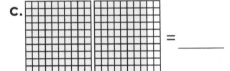 = _____

3. Write each fraction as a percentage.

a. $\dfrac{19}{100}$ = _____ **b.** $\dfrac{32}{100}$ = _____

c. $\dfrac{84}{100}$ = _____ **d.** $\dfrac{70}{100}$ = _____

e. $\dfrac{1}{2}$ = _____ **f.** $\dfrac{3}{4}$ = _____

4. Find the new price after the discount.

a. 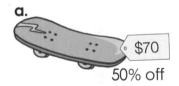 $70
50% off

New price_____

b.  $120
25% off

New price_____

5. Find each new total.

a. 80 less 25%_____ **b.** 60 less 75% _____

c. 100 less 52%_____ **d.** 50 less 10% _____

50 **e.** 20 less 30% _____ **f.** 48 less 25% _____

---

1. Add the fractions.
NB. Each one has the same denominator

a. $\dfrac{1}{4} + \dfrac{1}{4} = $ — **b.** $\dfrac{3}{10} + \dfrac{1}{10} = $ — **c.** $\dfrac{3}{8} + \dfrac{1}{8} = $

d. $\dfrac{1}{10} + \dfrac{7}{10} = $ — **e.** $\dfrac{1}{5} + \dfrac{2}{5} = $ — **f.** $\dfrac{1}{3} + \dfrac{1}{3} = $

2. Find the difference between the fractions
NB. Each one has the same denominator

a. $\dfrac{7}{8} - \dfrac{3}{8} = $ — **b.** $\dfrac{7}{10} - \dfrac{3}{10} = $ — **c.** $\dfrac{7}{9} - \dfrac{2}{9} = $

d. $\dfrac{5}{6} - \dfrac{1}{6} = $ — **e.** $\dfrac{9}{10} - \dfrac{3}{10} = $ — **f.** $\dfrac{4}{5} - \dfrac{1}{5} = $

3. Write the equivalent fraction for each one

a. $\dfrac{2}{5} = \dfrac{⬭}{10}$ **b.** $\dfrac{3}{4} = \dfrac{⬭}{8}$ **c.** $\dfrac{1}{2} = \dfrac{⬭}{4}$

d. $\dfrac{1}{3} = \dfrac{⬭}{9}$ **e.** $\dfrac{4}{5} = \dfrac{⬭}{10}$ **f.** $\dfrac{2}{3} = \dfrac{⬭}{6}$

g. $\dfrac{3}{5} = \dfrac{⬭}{10}$ **h.** $\dfrac{1}{4} = \dfrac{⬭}{8}$ **i.** $\dfrac{1}{4} = \dfrac{⬭}{12}$

4. Add the fractions. To add change one fraction so both have the same denominator

a. $\dfrac{2}{3} + \dfrac{1}{6} = $

$\dfrac{}{6} + \dfrac{}{6} = \dfrac{}{⬭}$

b. $\dfrac{2}{5} + \dfrac{3}{10} = $

$\dfrac{}{10} + \dfrac{}{10} = $ —

c. $\dfrac{5}{8} + \dfrac{1}{4} = $

$\dfrac{}{8} + \dfrac{}{8} = \dfrac{}{⬭}$

d. $\dfrac{3}{8} + \dfrac{1}{2} = $

$\dfrac{}{8} + \dfrac{}{8} = $ —

Symmetry

Colour the shapes that will tessellate.

a. 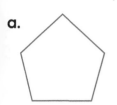   b.   c.

d.   e.   f.

g.   h.   i.

Draw lines of symmetry on each shape and then count and record them.

a.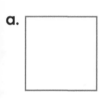

b.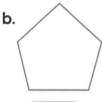

Lines of symmetry

Lines of symmetry

Draw the other half of each shape.

a.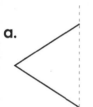

b.

What shapes have been used in this pattern? Colour the pattern.

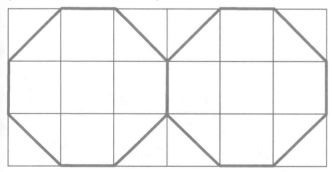

Shapes used _____

_____

Data

1. Here is a picture graph showing the sale of coffee in a shop for one week.

Key ☕ = 10

Days	Customers
Monday	☕☕
Tuesday	☕☕☕
Wednesday	☕☕☕☕
Thursday	☕☕☕☕☕☕
Friday	☕☕☕
Saturday	☕☕☕☕☕☕
Sunday	☕☕☕☕☕☕☕☕☕

Sales of Coffee

a. How many customers on the quietest day had coffee?

b. Which day would need extra staff?

_____

c. How many cups of coffee were sold on Wednesday?

d. How many more cups of coffee were sold on Sunday than on Saturday?

e. How many cups of coffee were sold over the whole week?

f. If coffee was $5 per cup, what was the total weekly revenue from coffee sales?   _____

2. Here are the tallies for flavoured milk shakes sold at the local take-away. Record the figures on a horizontal graph.

Vanilla	Caramel	Chocolate	Strawberry
卌 卌 卌 l	卌 llll	卌 卌 卌 卌	卌 卌 lll

ICE CREAMS

Vanilla

Caramel

Chocolate

Strawberry

5   10   15   20

Calculator and Patterns

1. Use your calculator to write the next three numbers in each pattern.

	Rule	Pattern
a.	x 3	4 132 _____ _____ _____
b.	+ 7	58 406 _____ _____ _____
c.	$\square^2$	25 _____ _____ _____
d.	+ 3 816	3 031 6 847 _____ _____ _____
e.	- 347	8 378 8 031 _____ _____ _____
f.	x 0.1	1 328 132.8 _____ _____ _____

2. Follow the path by calculating each step and fill in the missing numbers.

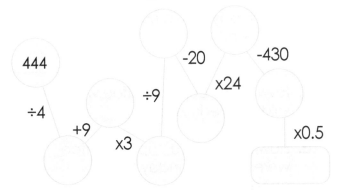

3. Complete each number sentence. Remember the order of operations.

a. (27x3)+(13x8)=_____ **b.** (62x2)+(14x8)=_____

c. (12x17)+(9x40)=_____ **d.** (39÷3)+(15x9)=_____

e. (18x18)-(12x9)=_____ **f.** (52+75)-86= _____

4. Multiply each decimal by 0.4

a. 24.3 _____   **b.** 35.6 _____

c. 8.07 _____   **d.** 0.95 _____

e. 17.66_____   **f.** 2.83 _____

5. Divide the numerator by the denominator to find an equivalent, decimal fraction.

a. $\dfrac{3}{6}$= _____   **b.** $\dfrac{1}{5}$= _____   **c.** $\dfrac{4}{5}$= _____

d. $\dfrac{6}{24}$= _____   **e.** $\dfrac{5}{8}$ = _____   **f.** $\dfrac{3}{4}$= _____

52

Multiplication

1. Complete each multiplication algorithm.

a. 27
34 x
_____

b. 48
23 x
_____

c. 42
36 x
_____

d. 75
25
_____

e. 56
32 x
_____

f. 63
27 x
_____

g. 127
19 x
_____

h. 235
2
_____

2. Problems:

a. There are 42 children in Year 5. Each had to pay $36 to go on a trip to Canberra. How much was collected by the teacher if everyone paid?

collected

b. The fruit shop had a pallet of apples. There were 64 boxes on the pallet. Each box contained 144, how many apples in total?

apples

3. Use your knowledge of multiplication to complete the cross number puzzle.

Across

1. 18 x 4 =

3. 27 x 3 =

5. 11 x 8 =

6. 5 x 7 =

10. 4 x ⬚ = 32

11. 77 x 4 =

Down

1. 2 x 36 =

2. 3 x 6 =

4. 2 x 9 =

6. 4 x 8 =

7. 7 x 9 =

8. 6 x 15 =

10. 17 x 5 =

Circles

Measure the radius of each circle.

a.

r =_____mm

b.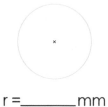

r =_____mm

c.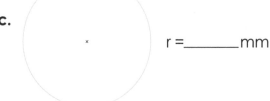

r =_____mm

Measure the diameter of each circle.

a.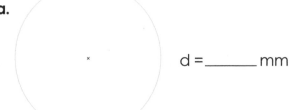

d =_____ mm

b. 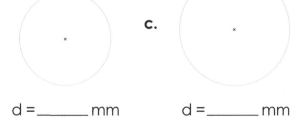 **c.**

d =_____ mm   d =_____ mm

Use a compass to draw a circle with a 25mm radius.

24 Hour Time

1. Write each pm time in digital form.

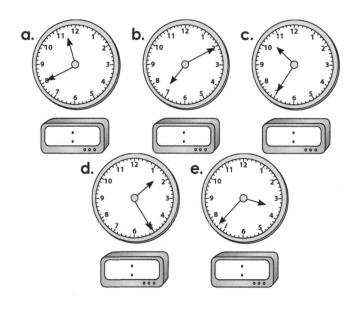

2. Write each time in 24 hour time.

a. 2:15p.m. _____ **b.** 1:10a.m._____

c. midnight_____ **d.** 10:55p.m._____

3. Write each 24 hour time as either am or pm time.

a. 1000 _____ **b.** 1350 _____

c. 0308 _____ **d.** 1205 _____

e. 0000 _____ **f.** 1455 _____

4. Write in 24 hour time each written time on the digital watch.

a. ten minutes to midday

b. lunch time

c. time I go to bed

d. quarter past midnight

e. half an hour before midnight

53

Credit card

1. List three things you can buy with an EFTPOS card.

   _____

   _____

   _____

2.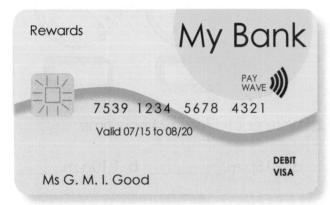

   a. What is the EFTPOS card number?

   _____

   b. Which bank issued the card?

   _____

   c. Whose name appears on the card?

   _____

   d. What does the))) symbol mean?

   _____

   e. When does this card expire?

   _____

3. All cards have a Personal Identification Number or PIN. Write a PIN for this card. _____

4. A statement is issued for all card holders. How often is a statement issued? _____

5. What does a statement show?

   _____

6. If the card is used as a credit card, how long does the cardholder have before interest is charged on the balance? _____

54 7. What is interest? _____

Division

1. Answer True (**T**) or False (**F**) for each stateme

   a. 846 is a multiple of 6 _____

   b. 5 is a factor of 90 _____

   c. 93 is a multiple of 9 _____

   d. 12 is a factor of 144 _____

   e. 107 is a multiple of 7 _____

   f. 8 is a factor of 60 _____

2. Complete each division in its contracted form. Write the remainder too.

   a. $8\overline{)967}$ r

   b. $4\overline{)893}$ r

   c. $5\overline{)62}$

   d. $4\overline{)683}$ r

   e. $9\overline{)640}$ r

   f. $7\overline{)85}$

3. Find the missing number in each sentence

   a. ☐ ÷ 7 = 12 r 1

   b. ☐ ÷ 5 = 16 r 2

   c. 145 ÷ 12 = ☐ r 1

   d. 135 ÷ 6 = ☐

   e. 800 ÷ 9 = ☐ r 8

   f. 427 ÷ ☐ = 85

4. Trade place values to complete each division in its contracted form.

   a. $7\overline{)4\,386}$ r

   b. $7\overline{)5\,142}$ r

   c. $5\overline{)3\,626}$

   d. $4\overline{)5\,315}$ r

   e. $5\overline{)2\,957}$ r

   f. $6\overline{)3\,386}$

3D Objects

me the 3D objects drawn from various
wpoints and projections.

1.

_____

2.

_____

3.

_____

4.

_____

5.

_____

6.
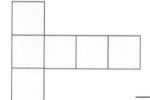
_____

7.

_____

8.
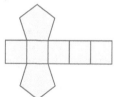
_____

9.

_____

10.
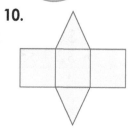
_____

Location

Use the map of Samson to answer
each question.

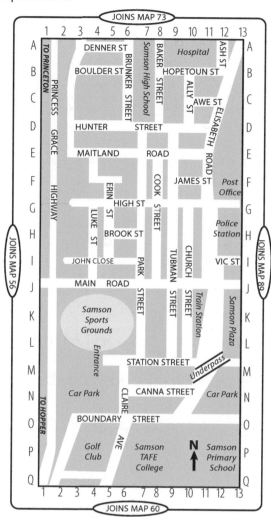

1. What is found at K4? _____

2. What landmark is found at F12? _____

3. What type of sporting ground is found
   south of the Sports Ground? _____

4. Give the co-ordinates for the
   primary school. _____

5. What is found at M10? _____

6. In what direction does
   Cook St run? _____

7. In what direction is the Police
   Station from the train station? _____

8. Give the co-ordinates for the
   intersection of Main Road and
   Princess Grace Highway. _____

9. What is north-east
   of the high school? _____

10. In which direction does
    Main Road run? _____

11. In which direction is Princeton? _____

12. What can be found at N12? _____ **55**

Multiples and Factors

1. Colour the multiples around the wheel for each centre number.

a.

19
91   63
48   **7**   28
21   49
53

b.

44
54   36
28   **9**   81
27   39
90

2. Write the multiple for each set of factors.

a. 9 and 9 = _____   **b.** 8 and 6 = _____

c. 12 and 7 = _____   **d.** 7 and 5 = _____

e. 5 and 11 = _____   **f.** 3 and 13 = _____

g. 8 and 6 = _____   **h.** 17 and 3 = _____

3. Write the factors for each number.

a. 15 ☐ , ☐ , ☐ and ☐

b. 24 ☐ , ☐ , ☐ , ☐ , ☐ , ☐ and ☐

c. 16 ☐ , ☐ , ☐ and ☐

d. 28 ☐ , ☐ , ☐ , ☐ and ☐

4. Answer True (**T**) or False (**F**) about the factors and multiples.

a. 7 is a factor of 77 _____

b. 81 is a multiple of 27 _____

c. 30 is a multiple of 10 _____

d. 6 is a factor of 84 _____

e. 51 is a multiple of 3 _____

f. 85 is a multiple of 5 _____

5. What number am I?

a. My factors are 1, 2, 4, 8 and 16 _____

b. My factors are 1, 2, 4, 5, 10 and 20 _____

c. My factors are 1, 2, 3, 4, 6, 9 and 18 _____

Addition

1. Add each group of numbers.

a. 6 324
8 137
+1 583
_____

b. 6 824
3 158
+6 267
_____

c. 2 4
6 9
+ 4 1
_____

2. Find the missing number in each sentence

a. 2 172 + ☐ + 5 327 = 10 366

b. 4 867 + 3 948 ☐ = 10 511

c. ☐ + 4 795 + 8 264 = 16 33

d. 3 728 + 5 419 + 6 263 = ☐

3. Complete the addition grid. A calculator will help.

+	6 244	3 519	7 395
4 273			
8 164			
5 144			
3 275			

4. Round off each number to the nearest thousand to find approximate totals. Check with a calculator.

a. 7 167 + 2 905 + 4 101 ≃ _____

Calculator Total _____

b. 3 954 + 2 132 + 5 060 ≃ _____

Calculator Total _____

c. 5 724 + 3 351 + 6 989 ≃ _____

Calculator Total _____

5. Add each sum of money.

a. $2 637. 25
+ $1 548. 78
_____

b. $6 257. 3
+ $2 183. 8
_____

Mass

Write the unit of mass used for each object.
(grams, kilograms or tonne)

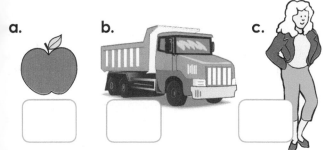

a.   b.   c.

d.   e.   f.

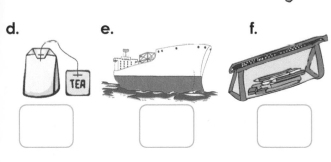

Find the mass.

a. A container has a mass of 11 grams when empty. When full its mass is 955 grams. What is the net mass? _____

b. Calculate the gross mass of a jar of jam if the jar is 18 grams and the jam is 425 grams. The gross mass is _____

c. Five coffee jars are full. The total mass is 2.5 kilograms. Each jar of coffee has a mass of 350 grams. What is the net mass of the jars?

_____

Find each gross mass.

a.  Jar's mass 125g

Gross mass _____

b.

Box's mass 7g

Gross mass _____

c.

Container 12g

Gross mass _____

d.  Bottle 15g

Gross mass _____

Transformation

1. Draw each shape after each transformation.

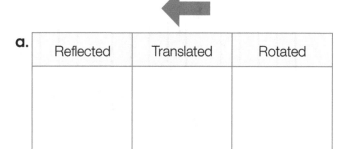

a.

Reflected	Translated	Rotated

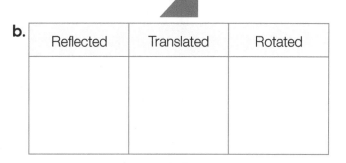

b.

Reflected	Translated	Rotated

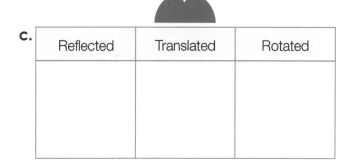

c.

Reflected	Translated	Rotated

2. Draw the new shape by reflecting each shape over its axis of symmetry.

a.   b.

c.   d.

3. Write the transformation for each pair of shapes.

a. _____

b. _____

c. _____

57

Place Value

1. Write the number represented on each abacus.

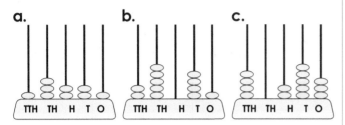

a.   b.   c.

| TTH TH H T O | TTH TH H T O | TTH TH H T O |

_____   _____   _____

2. In each, arrange the numerals to make the smallest number.

a. 4 2 1 6 7   b. 8 2 5 1 7   c. 3 0 5 2 6

_____   _____   _____

d. 7 8 3 1 2   e. 5 3 1 2 4   f. 8 5 0 7 0

_____   _____   _____

3. Write the number which is 3 120 less than that on each card.

a.
TTH	TH	H	T	O
IIII	III	IIII		III

_____

b.
TTH	TH	H	T	O
IIIIIII		III	IIIII	III

_____

c.
TTH	TH	H	T	O
III	IIIII	IIII	II	IIII

_____

4. Identify the place value for each circled number.

a. 4 5 . ③ 7 2 _____

b. 8 6 5 . 4 ⑤ _____

c. ⑥ 5 3 9 . 4 0 _____

d. 3 3 ⑤ . 2 7 _____

5. How many tens in 68 374?   _____

6. How many thousands in 83 217? _____

58 **7.** How many hundreds in 66 753? _____

Adding and Subtracting Decimals

1. Add each group of decimals.

a.   42.73   b.   436.22   c.   721.
       125.51   59.77   612.
      +662.39   +138.29   + 99.

_____   _____   _____

2. Subtract these decimal fractions.

a.   b.   c.
   537.65   674.81   73.
 - 114.33   - 143.67   - 9.

_____   _____   _____

3. Add the decimals.

a. 42.65 + 321.77 + 68.45 = _____

b. 586.29 + 38.66 + 153.70 = _____

c. 402.35 + 166.74 + 38.09 = _____

d. 888.43 + 217.45 + 162.04 = _____

4. Find the difference between the decimals

a. 827.45 - 172.49 = _____

b. 365.88 - 227.99 = _____

c. 750.62 - 332.48 = _____

5. Problems:

a. A runner ran a marathon in 4 hours, 8 minutes, 42 seconds. His friend ran it in hours 29 minutes, 38 seconds. What wo the difference in the times?

_____

b. How much timber is needed to fence property 32.75m by 42.45m. The prope is a true rectangle.
The timber needed is _____

Angles

Draw each angle.

a. right angle

b. acute angle

c. obtuse angle

Write the size of each angle showing on the protractor.

a.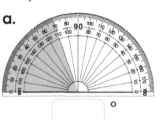

◯ °

b.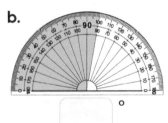

◯ °

c.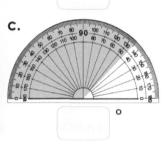

◯ °

d.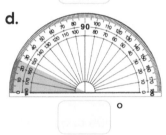

◯ °

Use a protractor to measure each angle.

a.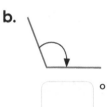

◯ °

b.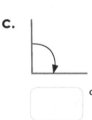

◯ °

c.

◯ °

Colour each angle on the protractor.

a. 140°

b. 50°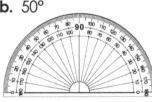

c. 90°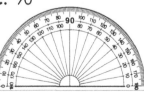

d. 110°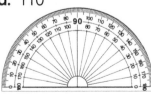

a. How many degrees in a right angle? _____

b. How many degrees in a straight angle? _____

Measuring Time

1. How much time has lapsed between that shown on each?

a.  a.m. 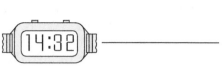 _____

b. p.m.  _____

c. p.m.  _____

2. Show each time on the stop watch.

a. 4 minutes 32 seconds 19 hundredths

b. 7 minutes 53 seconds 62 hundredths

c. 10 minutes 19 seconds 48 hundredths

d. 1 minutes 38 seconds 90 hundredths

3. A stopwatch shows 2:27:52. What does this mean?

_____

4. Order the times, shortest to longest.

8 : 14 : 32, 8 : 40 : 36, 6 : 19 : 27, 7 : 14 : 33

_____

5. Josie won her race. Her time was 3:09:37. She was 4 seconds faster than second place. What was the time for second place? _____

6. Two stopwatches showed 9:11:08 and 9:11:15 for the same race. What is the difference?

_____

59

Answers

Unit 1

Division: 1a. 10 **b.** 9 **c.** 8 **d.** 8   **2a.** 28 ÷ 4 = 7 **b.** 39 ÷ 3 = 13 **c.** 24 ÷ 6 = 4   **3a.** 5 **b.** 8 **c.** 4 **d.** 6 **e.** 11 **f.** 12   **4a.** 8 **b.** 5 **c.** 32 **d.** 7
Decimal Fractions: 1a. 0.6 **b.** 0.3 **c.** 0.7 **d.** 0.9   **2a.** 7/10 **b.** 3/10 **c.** 9/10   **d.** 2/10 **e.** 6/10 **f.** 5/10 **g.** 4/10 **h.** 1/10 **3a.** 0.5 **b.** 0.9 **c.** 0.3 **d.** 2/10 **e.** 7/10 **f.** 0.25 **g.** 0.8 **h.** 6/10 or 3/5
4. colour - **a.** 5 squares **b.** 6 squares **c.** 8 squares **d.** 3 squares **e.** 2 squares
Length: 1a. 3.0m **b.** 2.58m **c.** 7.5m **d.** 1.72m **e.** 13.6m **f.** 123.0m **2.** parent **3a.** 11 cm **b.** 14 cm **4a.** cm **b.** cm **c.** m **d.** mm **e.** cm
Shopping: 1a. $20.89 **2.** $60 **3.** $80 **4a.** $28 **b.** $31 **c.** $60.05 **d.** $21.50 **5.** 34 **6.** 240

Unit 2

Place Value: 1a. 34 155 **b.** 13 563 **c.** 70 673 **2a.** thousands **b.** hundreds **c.** tens of thousands **d.** hundreds **3a.** 64 276 **b.** 72 942 **c.** 38 751 **d.** 92 067 **4a.** 32 651 **b.** 72 635
5. Twenty seven thousand, three hundred and eighty six.
Multiplication: 1a. 2 464 **b.** 9 366 **c.** 4 888 **2a.** 48 **b.** 45 **c.** 90 **d.** 51 **3a.** 750 mL **b.** 2 465 x 2 = 4 9
4. 180, 810, 450, 2 700, 900, 630, 540, 90 **5a.** 84 **b.** 36 **c.** 120 **d.** 75
Area: 1a. 12 cm² **b.** 11 cm² **2a.** 600 cm2 **b.** 375 cm² **c.** 2 m² **d.** 3.75 m² **e.** 150 cm² **3a.** 30 cm² **b.** 2 cm² **c.** 32 cm² **d.** 60 cm² **4.** 6 cm²
Time: 1a. 06:30 **b.** 19:45 **c.** 20:20 **d.** 09:15 **e.** 16:40 **f.** 15:50 **2a.** 21:18 **b.** 15:45 **c.** 13:40 **d.** 22:27 **e.** 23:07 **3a.** 8:00 pm **b.** 4:45 pm **c.** 5:56 pm **d.** 11:40 pm **e.** 2:45 pm **f.** 1:27 pm **g.** 8:56 am **h.** 6:42 a

Unit 3

Subtraction: 1a. 413 **b.** 555 **c.** 434 **d.** 222 **2a.** 3 227 **b.** 5 725 **c.** 5 253 **d.** 2 636 **3.** 5 256
4a. 53, 264, 146, 255, 842, 437 **4b.** 34, 245, 127, 236, 823, 418 **4c.** 45, 256, 138, 247, 834, 429
Percentages: 1a. 72% **b.** 53% **c.** 38% **d.** 24% **e.** 77% **f.** 20% **g.** 36% **h.** 40% **2a.** 36% **b.** 67% **c.** 13% **d.** 79% **3a.** 74% **b.** 85% **c.** 32% **d.** 68% **e.** 6% **f.** 50% **4a.** 0.75, 75% **b.** 4/10, 40% **c.** 32/100, 0.32, **d.** 0.9, 90% **e.** ¼, 25%
Volume: 1a. 12 **b.** 10 **c.** 10 **d.** 27 **2a.** 32 cm3 **b.** 36 cm³
Probability: 1a. 0, **b.** teacher **c.** 0.5 **d.** teacher **e.** 1 **f.** 0.5 **2a.** 0.25 **b.** 0.25 **c.** 0.25 **d.** 0.25 **3.** b **4.** c **5.** parent **6.** parent

Unit 4

Addition: 1a. 107 **b.** 108 **c.** 189 **d.** 338 **2a.** 8 665 **b.** 7 695 **c.** 6 692 **d.** 8 443 **3a.** 30 **b.** 33 **c.** 123 **d.** 40, 53, 33, 60, 186 **4.** 100 **5.** 119 **6.** 1 174 **7.** 2 221
Factors and Multiples: 1a. 1, 2, 3, 4, 6, 12 **b.** 1, 3, 5, 15 **c.** 1, 2, 4, 5, 10, 20 **d.** 1, 3, 13, 39
2a. True **b.** True **c.** True **d.** False **3a.** 27, 81, 18 **b.** 36, 42 **c.** 14, 35, 56 **d.** 32, 56, 80
4a. 3, 6, 9, 12, 15, 18 **b.** 7, 14, 21, 28, 35, 42 **c.** 5, 10, 15, 20, 25, 30 **d.** 9, 18, 27, 36, 45, 54 **e.** 4, 12, 16, 20, 24
Capacity: 1a. 3 500mL **b.** 500mL **c.** 1 000mL **d.** 2 250mL **e.** 2 500mL **f.** 5 250mL **2a.** 700mL **b.** 500mL **c.** 850mL **3a.** 3 750mL **b.** 3 100mL **4a.** 0.375 **b.** 0.6 **c.** 0.4 **d.** 0.75 **e.** 0.25 **f.** 1.35
Location: 1. B10 **2.** C4 **3.** D9 **4.** E2 **5.** B6 **6.** G10 **7.** A2 **8.** H5 **9.** H3 **10.** C8 **2a.** B4 **b.** F5 **c.** E3 **d.** A1 **e.** C2 **f.** D5 **g.** E1 **h.** F2 **i.** D4 **j.** A5 **k.** A3 **l.** C5

Unit 5

Rounding off: 1a. 80 **b.** 100 **c.** 50 **d.** 80 **e.** 30 **f.** 40 **g.** 50 **h.** 20 **i.** 90 **2a.** $2.35 **b.** $5.00 **c.** $10.45 **d.** $7.20 **e.** $12.55 **f.** $8.80 **3a.** 8 000 **b.** 5 000 **c.** 3 000 **d.** 4 000 **e.** 4 000 **f.** 4 000
4a. 800 **b.** 400 **c.** 1 500 **5.** $13
Patterns: 1a. ÷5 **b.** double **c.** x 10 **d.** x 3 **2a.** 0.6 **b.** 4/10 **c.** 3/8, ¾ **d.** 6.0 **e.** 5/6
3a. 38, 13, 23, 28, 43, 18 **b.** 16, 26, 78, 42, 18, 34 **c.** 1, 16, 22, 34, 19, 13
Angles: 1a. obtuse, **b.** reflex **c.** right **d.** acute
2a. acute angle **b.** straight angle **c.** obtuse angle **d.** reflex angle **3a.** acute **b.** obtuse **c.** straight
Temperature: 1a. b. c. d. parent **2a.** 100°C **b.** 42°C **c.** 65°C **d.** 0°C **e.** 37°C
3a. 50°C **b.** 26°C **c.** 60°C **4a.** twenty-seven degrees Celsius **b.** ten degrees Celsius **c.** zero degrees Celsius **d.** ninety-four degrees Celsius

Unit 6

Division: 1a. 5 r1 **b.** 3 r1 **c.** 3 r2 **2a.** 5 **b.** 4 **c.** 5 **d.** 4 **e.** 7 **f.** 7 **3a.** 13r1 **b.** 12r1 **c.** 6r2 **d.** 8r2 **e.** 22r1 **f.** 12r3 **4.** 11 cartons 4 left over
Fractions: 1a. 2.5 **b.** 0.4 **c.** 5% **d.** 1/3 **2a.** 2/6 **b.** 5/10 **c.** 4/8 **d.** 1/3 **e.** 8/12 **f.** 6/10 **g.** ¼ **h.** 6/8 **i.** ½
3a. 0.5 **b.** 0.8 **c.** 0.75 **d.** 0.4 **e.** 0.2 **f.** 0.7 **4a.** $63 **b.** $18 **c.** $45 **d.** $72 **5a.** $33 **b.** $66 **c.** $44 **d.** $55
2D Shapes: 1a. square **b.** rectangle **c.** pentagon **d.** hexagon **e.** triangle **f.** trapezium **g.** rhombus **2a.** octagon **b.** scalene triangle **3a.** 2 **b.** 4
Transformation: 1. parent **2.** parent **3.** 1/2

Answers

Unit 7

Tables: a. x2 = 0, 2, 4, 6, 8, 10, 12, 14, 16, 18, 20 **b.** x3 = 0, 3, 6, 9, 12, 15, 18, 21, 24, 27, 30 **c.** x4 = 0, 4, 8, 12, 16, 20, 24, 28, 32, 36, 40 **d.** x5 = 0, 5, 10, 15, 20, 25, 30, 35, 40, 45, 50 **e.** x6 = 0, 6, 12, 18, 24, 30, 36, 42, 48, 54, 60 **f.** x7 = 0, 7, 14, 21, 28, 35, 42, 49, 56, 63, 70 **g.** x8 = 0, 8, 16, 24, 32, 40, 48, 56, 64, 72, 80 **h.** x9 = 0, 9, 18, 27, 36, 45, 54, 63, 72, 81, 90 **i.** x10 = 0, 10, 20, 30, 40, 50, 60, 70, 80, 90, 100

Multiplication: 1a. 28 **b.** 69 **c.** 80 **d.** 155 **e.** 96 **f.** 700 **g.** 2 700 **h.** 3 000 **2a.** 4 648 **b.** 5 408 **c.** 6 489 **d.** 13 230 **e.** 9 268 **f.** 8 638 **3.** 1 160 **4a.** $86.40 **b.** $407.25 **c.** $195.00 **5a.** 24,30,36,90,60 **b.** 56, 70, 84, 210, 140

Nets: 1. cylinder **2.** square pyramid **3.** cube **4.** hexagonal pyramid **5.** cone **6.** pentagonal prism **7.** hexagonal prism

Graphs: 1. 80 **2.** Monday **3.** 5 **4.** Monday **5.** Saturday **6.** It's the week-end and the factory would only work half a day. OR It is the day the least number of dresses are made. **7.** Tuesday & Friday **8.** 30 dresses **9.** 490 dresses

Unit 8

Problems: 1. 99÷3=33, **2.** 3, **3.** 48, **4.** 2 505kms **5.** 4, **6.** $66.20 **7.** $33.80

Multiples and Factors: 1a. 1, 2, 3, 6, 9, 18, **b.** 1, 2, 4, 5, 10, 20 **c.** 1, 2, 3, 4, 6, 12 **d.** 1, 2, 5, 10 **2a.** 6, 9, 12, 15, 18 **b.** 4, 6, 8, 10,12 **c.** 10,15, 20, 25, 30 **d.** 8,12,16, 20, 24 **e.** 12, 18, 24, 30, 36 **3a.** 20 **b.** 63 **c.** 54 **d.** 40 **e.** 21 **f.** 42 **g.** 45 **h.** 80 **4a.** 7, **b.** 13, **c.** 55, **d.** 12, **e.** 8, **f.** 12 **5a.** true **b.** true **c.** false

Mass: 1a. 42kg **b.** 38kg **c.** 43kg **d.** 27kg **2a.** 4 tonne **b.** 895 kilograms **c.** 2 kilograms **d.** 500 grams **3a.** 0.835kg **b.** 1.25kg **c.** 0.165kg **d.** 2kg **e.** 1.5kg **f.** 2.235kg

24 Hour Time: 1a. 16:45 **b.** 13:40 **c.** 19:55 **d.** 14:50 **e.** 18:10 **f.** 20:20 **2a.** 18:30 **b.** 08:45 **c.** 16:35 **d.** 19:56 **3a.** ⊙ **b.** ⊙ **c.** ⊙ **4a.** 19:16 **b.** 15:05 **c.** 12:10

Unit 9

Subtraction: 1a. 5 711 **b.** 6 251 **c.** 4 442 **d.** 5 221 **e.** 3 532 **f.** 4 113 **2a.** 6 118 **b.** 6 201 **c.** 2 129 **d.** 5 413 **e.** 5 318 **f.** 2 559 **3a.** $311.28 **b.** $330.77 **4a.** 6 124 **b.** 1 757

Multiplying by 10s and 100s: 1a. 6 240 **b.** 3 450 **c.** 87 520 **d.** 83 500 **e.** 513 100 **f.** 623 300 **2a.** 327.2 **b.** 415.3 **c.** 836.6 **d.** 8336 **e.** 4555 **f.** 1736 **3a.** $23.30 **b.** $17.50 **c.** 2220 runs **4a.** 213.2, 427, 186.2, 513.8 **b.** 2132,4270,1862,5138 **5.** 3 750mL

Tessellation: 1. colour - a., c., d., e., g., i., j., l. **2.** Parent **3.** draw a.-f., b.-e., c.-h., d.-g.

GST: 1a. $75.90 **b.** $90.20 **c.** $511.50 **d.** $48.40 **e.** $913 **f.** $69.30 **2.** colour - a.,b.,e. **3a.** $3 505 **b.** $350.50 **c.** $3 855.50

Unit 10

Addition: 1a. 5 697 **b.** 7 897 **c.** 7 877 **2a.** 7 942 **b.** 5 765 **c.** 5 845 **d.** 6 737 **e.** 7 904 **f.** 6 825 **3a.** 182 **b.** 289 **c.** 251 **d.** 314 **e.** 45 **f.** 70 **g.** 602 **h.** 411 **4a.** 1 312 **b.** 2 787 **c.** 1 300 **d.** 506 **e.** 582

Equivalent Fractions: 1. 3/10 **2.** 7/8 **3.** 1/5, 3/10, 1/2, 3/5, 7/10, 4/5 **4a.** 4/8 **b.** 1/5 **c.** 2/4 **d.** 2/12 **e.** 2/8 **f.** 1/3 **5a.** ½ **b.** ¼ **c.** 3/5 **d.** ¾ **e.** 1/5 **f.** ¼ **6a.** 7/10 **b.** 1/4 **c.** 3/10 **d.** 8/10 **e.** ½ **f.** ¾ **7a.** ¾ **b.** 5/6 **c.** 8/10 OR 4/5

Polygons: 1a. square **b.** trapezium **c.** pentagon **d.** rectangle **e.** hexagon **f.** right angle triangle **2a.** 3 **b.** 2 **c.** 2 **d.** 5 **3a.** false **b.** true **c.** false **d.** true **e.** true

Timetables: 1a. 23:18 ⊙ **b.** 06:40 ⊙ **c.** 12:10 ⊙ **d.** 00:52 ⊙ **2a.** 4 mins **b.** 1hr 17 mins **c.** 3 mins **d.** 13:15 **e.** 14:05 **f.** 1 hr 40min

Unit 11

Place Value: 1a. 82 965 **b.** 74 278 **c.** 63 856 **d.** 94 079 **2a.** 87 678 **b.** 22 945 **c.** 54 392 **d.** 61 578 **e.** 40 251 **3a.** 325 417 **b.** 162 108 **c.** 611 340 **d.** 204 065 **4a.** thousands **b.** hundreds **c.** hundreds **d.** thousands

Decimals: 1. - in order on line - 0.3, 0.4, 0.5, 0.7, 0.8, 0.9, 1.1, 1.2, 1.6, 1.9 **2a.** 0.5 **b.** 2.3 **c.** 1.7 **d.** 0.75 **e.** 1.0 **f.** 1.0 **3a.** 0.3, 0.5 **b.** 1.7, 2.3 **c.** 1.5,1.4,1.3 **4a.** 3.2 **b.** 2.8 **c.** 2.9 **d.** 4.1 **e.** 4.3 **f.** 1.5 **5a.** 0.2, 0.3, 0.5, 0.6, 0.8, 0.9 **b.** 0.5, 0.7, 1.3, 1.6, 2.1, 2.4

Measuring Angles: 1 b **2a.** 75º **b.** 120º **c.** 30º **d.** 45º **3a.** straight **b.** obtuse **c.** right angle **d.** acute **e.** obtuse **f.** reflex **4a. b.** parent check

Line Graphs: 1. 40 kms **2.** 9 am **3.** Half an hour **4.** 4 hours **5.** 10:30am **6.** 11 a.m **7.** 1 hour **8.** 100 kms **9.** Parent **10.** 1-1/2 hours **11.** 2pm

Unit 12

Round Off: 1a. 76 000 **b.** 12 000 **c.** 82 000 **d.** 48 000 **e.** 27 000 **f.** 25 000 **2a.** 647 300 **b.** 599 000 **c.** 227 760 000 **d.** 97 082 000 **3a.** 10 300, 10 129 **b.** 7 000, 7 135 **c.** 12 100, 12 123 **d.** 2 900, 2 927 **4a.** 13 dozen **b.** 75 **c.** 73 or 74

Square Numbers: 1. match - a. - 4, b. -16, c. - 25, d. - 36, e. - 9, f. - 49 **2.** match a. - 225, b. - 121, c. - 64, d. - 400, e. - 144, f. - 81 **3a.** 97, b. 55, c. 44, d. 53, e. 50, f. 45 **4a.** 256, b. 441, c. 169, d. 900, e. 625, f. 324 **5.** 25

Perimeter: 1. 12 cm **2.** 12 cm **3.** 12 cm **4.** 7 cm **5.** 10 cm **6.** 12 cm **7.** 12 cm

Location: 1a. Swim Centre **b.** Barton St **c.** School **d.** Main Street **e.** Hospital **f.** Supermarket **g.** Church **h.** Chemist **i.** Joshua Close **j.** Police Station **k.** Oval **l.** Opera Hall **2a.** - g. parent **h.** movie theatre. **3.** Parent **4.** Parent.

Answers

Unit 13

Multiplication: 1a. x3 = 0, 3, 6, 9, 12, 15, 18, 21, 24, 27, 30 **b.** x4 = 0, 4, 8, 12, 16, 20, 24, 28, 32, 36, 40 **c.** x6 = 0, 6, 12, 18, 24, 30, 36, 42, 48, 54, 60 **d.** x7 = 0, 7, 14, 21, 28, 35, 42, 49, 56, 63, 7 **e.** x8 = 0, 8, 16, 24, 32, 40, 48, 56, 64, 72, 80 **f.** x9 = 0, 9, 18, 27, 36, 45, 54, 63, 72, 81, 90 **2a.** 620 **b.** 7 800 **c.** 98 000 **d.** 16 660 **e.** 42 860 **f.** 57 200 **3.** $1 000
Order of Operations: 1a. 21 **b.** 13 **c.** 13 **d.** 36 **e.** 29 **f.** 3 **g.** 33 **h.** 28 **2a.** 11 **b.** 4 **c.** 19 **d.** 18 **e.** 13 **f.** 27 **3a.** 15 **b.** 51 **c.** 21 **d.** 13 **e.** 0 **4 b** 2x24
Capacity: 1a. 250mL **b.** 220L **c.** 1250mL **d.** 25mL **e.** 4L **f.** 5mL **2a.** 600mL **b.** 350mL **c.** 750mL **3.** Parent **4.** Colour c
Temperature: 1a. parent **2.** 75°C **3.** 95°C **4.** parent **5a.** 62°C **b.** 0°C **c.** 100°C **d.** 37°C **e.** parent **6a.** 35°C **b.** 7°C **c.** 23°C

Unit 14

Division with Remainders: 1a. 8 r 1 **b.** 7r2 **c.** 7r5 **d.** 8r2 **e.** 5r2 **f.** 8r3 **g.** 17r1 **h.** 6r3 **i.** 8r3 **2a.** 27 **b.** 12 **c.** 1 **d.** r1 **3a.** 33r2 **b.** 123r1 **c.** 105r3 **d.** 57r4 **e.** 55r7 **f.** 113r1 **4.** 9r6 **5a.** r1 **b.** r2
Decimal Fractions: 1a. 0.5 **b.** 0.25 **c.** 0.4 **d.** 0.7 **e.** 0.1 **f.** 0.6 **g.** 0.75 **h.** 0.9 **i.** 0.2 **2a.** 0.9 **b.** 1.1 **c.** 7.6 **d.** 8.2 **e.** 10.9 **3a.** 0.4, 0.7 **b.** 1.0, 1.3 **c.** 0.7, 0.9 **4a.** 0.1, 0.4, 0.7, 0.9, 1.3, 1.8 **b.** 3.05, 3.15, 3.2, 3.25, 3.5, 3.55
Mass: 1a. 4.0kg **b.** 2.5kg **c.** 8.75kg **d.** 5.25kg **e.** 8.2kg **f.** 6.5kg **g.** 1.5kg **h.** 3.25kg **2a.** 90g **b.** 38kg **c.** 8T **d.** 20T **e.** 15g **f.** 2kg **3a.** 90g **b.** parent **c.** 600g **4a.** 32g **b.** 20g **c.** 30g
Ordering Time: 1a. 1:00pm **b.** 7:00am **c.** 4:30pm **d.** 9:00am **e.** 6:30pm **f.** 11:00am **g.** 8:00am **h.** 9:30pm **i.** 7:15am **j.** 3:00pm **2.** b, i, g, d, f, a, j, c, e, h **3a.** 2hrs 30 mins **b.** 2hrs 0mins50sec **c.** 0hr,11mins,20sec **d.** 6hrs10mins **4a.** 10 years **b.** 80-90 mins **c.** 14 days **d.** 20 seconds

Unit 15

Plus and Minus: 1a. 5 000 **b.** 4 000 **c.** 4 000 **d.** 6 000 **e.** 3 000 **f.** 5 000 **2a.** 6 000, 5 964 **b.** 8 000, 8 032 **c.** 9 000, 9000 **d.** 10 000, 10 100 **3a.** 2 000, 1 951 **b.** 7 000, 7 018 **c.** 2 000, 2 068 **d.** 5 000, 4 899 **4a.** 1 596 **b.** 7 320 **c.** Eight hundred and fifty six
Patterns & Rules: 1a. 341, 1 365 **b.** 72, 81 **c.** 16, 8 **d.** 59, 52 **e.** 540, 1 626 **2a.** 23, Rule=+4 **b.** 32 Rule=double **c.** 3 Rule=÷3 **d.** 162 Rule=X3 **e.** 2.785 Rule=÷10 **3a.** 1.5, 1.7 **b.** 6.5, 7.8 **c.** 9.2, 8.7 **d.** 10.6, 10.3 **e.** 10.4, 11.3 **4a.** 3.265 **b.** 3265 **c.** 24 600 **d.** 0.1875 **e.** 1 560 **f.** 0.729
Distance: 1. **2a.** NW **b.** Waxton **c.** 8 km **d.** C9 **e.** SE **f.** 14km **g.** 28km
GST: 1a. $104.50 **b.** $52.80 **c.** $93.50 **2.** Goods and Services Tax **3a.** $5 **b.** $3 **c.** $6 **d.** $120 **4a.** No **b.** Yes **c.** Yes **d.** Yes **e.** Yes **f.** Yes and No **5.** $39 **6.** Yes

Unit 16

Problems: 1. $13 026.00 **2.** $13 338.00 **3.** 56 pages **4.** 72 **5.** 2 kg @ $10 **6.** $257.50 **7.** 388 sheep **8.** $1 per kg cheaper.
Fractions: 1a. 0.27 **b.** 0.9 **c.** 0.8 **d.** 0.8 **e.** 0.5 **f.** 0.25 **g.** 0.44 **h.** 0.2 **i.** 0.3 **2a.** water sports **b.** 50% **c.** 25% **d.** cricket & netball **e.** 10 **f.** 5 **g.** 5 **3.** circle **a.** 2/10 **b.** 3/4 **c.** 1/3 **d.** 4/20 **e.** 0.6 **f.** 0.1
Flip, Slide, Turn: 1a. **b.** **c.** **d.** **2a.** slide turn or flip **b.** turn **c.** flip **d.** turn **3a.** 3 **b.** 4 **c.** 5 **d.** 1 **e.** 2 **Time: 1a.** **b.** **c.** **d.** **e.** **f.** **2a.** 06:30 **b.** 03:30 **c.** 01:15 **d.** 22:35 **e.** 20:50 **f.** 17:30 **3a.** 6:14am **b.** 10:10pm **c.** 10:40am **d.** 2:59pm **e.** 1:22pm **f.** 5:19pm

Unit 17

Factors: 1a. 1,2,6 **b.** 2,7,28 **2a.** 42 **b.** 32 **c.** 24 **d.** 35 **e.** 54 **f.** 24 **g.** 56 **h.** 33 **3a.** T **b.** T **c.** F **d.** T **e.** F **f.** T **4a.** 8 **b.** 8 **c.** 24 **d.** 14 **e.** 12 **f.** 27 **g.** 12. **h.** 8
Multiplication: 1a. 1 068 **b.** 981 **c.** 504 **d.** 928 **e.** 685 **f.** 2 430 **2a.** 80, 72, 48, 100, 40, 60 **b.** 48, 16, 56, 64, 32, 40, 24, 72 **3a.** 1L 500mL **b.** 5 250m or 5.25km **4a.** 9 642 **b.** 24 528 **c.** 16 780 **d.** 4 936 **e** 19 032 **f.** 37 688
Length: 1a. 80mm **b.** 65mm **c.** 50mm **d.** 85mm **2.** table = 10mm = 1 cm; 100cm = 1m; 1 000m = 1 km; **a.** 30cm **b.** 4 000m **c.** 50 000cm **d.** 1 000 cm **3a.** 105mm **b.** 10cm **4a.** 1m85cm **b.** 3m57cm **c.** 10m 38cm **d.** 4m 70cm **Chance: 1a.** 1/6 **b.** ½ **c.** 1/3 **d.** 1/5 **e.** ¼ **f.** 1/8 **2** parent **3a.** ½ **b.** ½ **c.** ¼ **d** 1/3

Unit 18

Rounding Off: 1a. 85c **b.** $1.10 **c.** $3.45 **d.** $7 **e.** $5.90 **f.** $6.45 **2.** **3a.** 8 000 **b.** 5 000 **c.** 5 000 **d.** 4 000 **e.** 5 000 **f.** 2 000 **4a.** $7 **b.** $9 **c.** $3 **d.** $11 **e.** $117 **f.** $869 **5a.** 1 200 **b.** 1 000 **c.** 1 000 **d.** 800
Division & Remainders: 1a. 55 r 2 **b.** 275r1 **c.** 96r1 **d.** 356r1 **e.** 42r3 **f.** 122r2 **2a.** 103r1 **b.** 104r3 **c.** 108r1 **d.** 109r2 **e.** 109r2 **f.** 105r5 **3a.** $171 each **b.** 25c x 4 = $1 **4a.** 3 **b.** 7 **c.** 5 **d.** 1 **e.** 0 **f.** 3
Area: 1a. m2 **b.** km2 **c.** m2 **d.** m2 **e.** ha **f.** km2 **2a.** 100 **b.** 3 000 m2 **c.** 80 **d.** 9 **e.** 5 **f.** 100 **3a.** P=220 m A=2 000 m2 **b.** P=290m A=3 200 m2
Line Graphs: 1. 30 **2.** June, August **3.** March **4.** 7 **5.** February **6.** July **7.** Yes **8.** March, December **9.** It's winter

Answers

Using a Calculator: 1a. 0.5 **b.** 0.25 **c.** 0.2 **d.** 0.66 **e.** 0.75 **f.** 0.3 **g.** 0.6 **h.** 0.375 **i.** 0.8
2a. 80% **b.** 70% **c.** 25% **d.** 87.5% OR 87 ½ % **e.** 40% **f.** 90% **g.** 20% **h.** 62.5% OR 62 ½ % **i.** 10%
3a. 50 **b.** 97 **c.** 78 **4a.** 71 **b.**123 **c.** 125 **d.** 175 **5a.** 448, 1 792 **b.** 80, 106 **c.** 16, 8
Addition: 1a. $61.90 **b.** $146.95 **c.** $230.24 **d.** $605.23 **e.** $ 1 097.65 **f.** $810.72
2a. 1 130 seats **b.** $265.10 **3a.** 2,1 **b.** 4,9 **c.** 5,3 **d.** 8,0 **e.** 4,4 **f.** 7,6
Volume: 1a. 90 **b.** 72 **c.** 60 **d.** 90 **e.** 80 **f.** 96 **2a.** 4x2x2=16 **b.** 5x2x3=30
3a. m3 **b.** cm3 **c.** mm3 **d.** m3 **e.** cm3 **4.** 7
Graphs & Charts: 1a. 12 **b.** 24 **c.** 6 **d.**12 **e.** 42 **2a.** 15 **b.** 10 **c.** 5 **d.** No **e.** cricket & netball **f.** 5 **g.** 40

Ordering Fractions: 1a. 0.47, 47% **b.** 0.8, 80% **c.** 0.7, 70% **d.** 0.75, 75% **e.** 0,25, 25% **f.** 0.79, 79%
2a. 0.09, 0.17, 0.36, 0.85, 0.92 **b.** 0.05, 0.47, 0.84, 1.02, 1.46 **c.** 0.89, 0.93, 1.24, 1.46, 2.98
3a. 3.68 **b.** 2.47 **c.** 8.09 **d.** 5.24 **4a.** 8.09, 5.24, 3.68, 2.47 **5a.** 0.6 **b.** 0.6 **c.** 0.75 **d.** 0.5
Subtraction: 1a. 5 312 **b.** 4 422 **c.** 2 251 **d.** 6 314 **e.** 7 315 **f.** 4 149 **2a.** 959 **b.** 2 907
3a. $212.32 **b.** $154.05 **c.** $621.34 **d.** $599.27 **e.** $419.03 **f.** $411.69 **4a.** 7,8, **b.** 2,3 **c.** 2,1
Capacity: 1a. L **b.** mL **c.** L **d.** mL **e.** mL **f.** L **2a.** 2 **b.** 3 **c.** 6 **d.** 3 640 **e.** 18 **f.** 9
3a. 15L 570mL **b.** 7L 475mL **c.** 12L 655mL **4a.** 1 500mL **b.** 5 540mL **c.** 2 350 mL **d.** 6 250 mL
e. 3 750 mL **f.** 4 500 mL
Chance: 1,2,3,4: parent check **5.** 1/6 **6a.** ¼ **b.** 1/5 **c.** 1/8 **d.** 1/10 **e.** 1/3 **f.** 1/8
7a. possible **b.** impossible **c.** possible

Equivalent Fractions: 1a. 2/10 **b.**1/25 **c.** 0.2 **d.** 6.0 **e.** ¾ **f.** 3/8 **2.** match **a.** - 25%, **b.** - 4/10, **c.** - 1/3,
d. - 0.5, **e.** - 75%, **f.** - 4/5, **3a.** 44%, 0.44, 44/100 **b.** 63%, 0.63, 63/100 **c.** 82%, 0.82, 82/100
4a. 2/4 **b.** 8/10 **c.** 3/5 **d.** 6/8 **e.** 5/10 **f.** 75/100
Decimal Fractions: 1a. 0.25, 0.4, 1.6, 1.75, 2.5, 2.8 **2a.** 0.15, 0.21, 0.35, 0.53, 0.62, 0.75 **b.** 0.75,
1.33, 1.47, 2.07, 2.68, 3.62 **c.** 0.16, 0.53, 0.55, 0.72, 1.09, 1.6 **3a.** 2.8 **b.** 1.65 **c.** 2.5 **d.** 1.4 **e.** 0.06
f. 0.5 **4a.** hundredths **b.** ones **c.** tenths **d.** tens **5a.** 174.21 **b.** 63.17 **c.** 316.07
Mass: 1. cow - 300 kg, girl - 45 kg, pumpkin - 5 kg, book - 2 kg, apple - 275g, cat - 3 kg, car - 2T,
pencil - 10g **2a.** 3 kg **b.** 4 ½ kg **c.** 10kg 200g **d.** 6 ½ kg **e.** 8 ½ kg **f.** 10 ¼ kg
3a. $168g^3$ **b.** $144g^3$ **c.** $180g^3$ **4a.** 2 160T **b.** $3.60
Time: 1a. 20:00 **b.** 18:55 **c.** 12:57 **d.** 14:28 **e.** 23:45 **2a.** seven thirty **b.** two twenty-five **c.** four fifteen
d. eleven forty-five **e.** one minute past twelve OR one minute past midnight **3a. b. c. d.** = parent
4a. 1788 **b.** 1901 **c.** 1914 **d.** 1915

Money: 1. colour - a, b, e, f, **2a.** $8 **b.** $4.50 **c.** $12 **d.** $1.80 **3a.** $79, $21 **b.** $80.50, $19.50
c. $76.95, $23.05 **4a.** $2 **b.** $8 **c.** $5 **d.** $19 **e.** $13 **f.** $65
Fractions: 1a. 4/10 **b.** 6/8 **c.** 5/10 **d.** 3/12 **e.** 2/6 **f.** 8/10 **2a.** 1/3 **b.** 3/5 **c.** ¾ **d.** ½ **e.** 7/10 **f.** ¼
3a. 2/8+3/8=5/8 **b.** 2/10+3/10=5/10 **c.** 1/8+2/8=3/8 **d.** 1/6+4/6=5/6 **e.** 4/10+5/10=9/10
4a. 7/8-2/8=5/8 **b.** 6/8-4/8=2/8 **c.** 7/8-4/8=3/8 **d.** 5/6-4/6=1/6 **e.** 5/10-2/10=3/10

Temperature: 1. a. 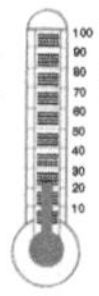 **b.** 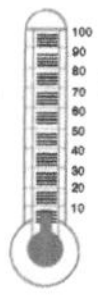 **c.** 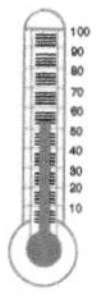 **d.** 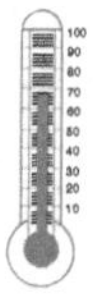 **e.** 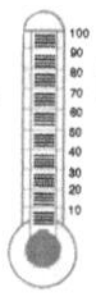 **f.** 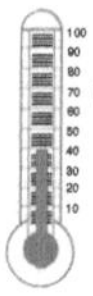 **g.** 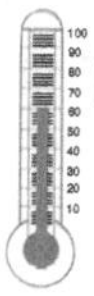 **h.**

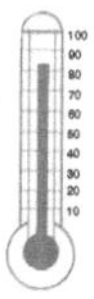

2a. 27 **b.** 0 **c.** 100 **d.** 20 **3.** autumn - 18°C, spring - 20°C, summer - 30°C, winter - 12°C **4a.** 40°C **b.**
18°C **c.** 12°C **d.** 20°C **e.** 35°C **f.** 20°C
Data Combinations: Row **1a.** chicken nuggets, fish and chips; hamburger Row **1b.** ice cream,
chocolate cake; ice cream, chocolate cake; ice cream, chocolate cake; **2.** 6 **3.** 12 **4.** Soup, chicken
nuggets, chocolate cake **5.** $15 **6.** Salad, hamburger, ice cream **7.** Strawberry/chocolate; chocolate/
vanilla; strawberry/vanilla; strawberry/strawberry; chocolate/chocolate; vanilla/vanilla

Order of Operations: 1a. 60 **b.** 138 **c.** 88 **d.** 45 **e.** 4 **f.** 30 **g.** 15 **h.** 5 **2a.** 41 **b.** 13 **c.** 58 **d.** 51 **3a.** 6 **b.**
9 **c.** 3 **d.** 2 **e.** 21 **f.** 9 **4a.** $10 **b.** $45 **c.** $15 **d.** $7 **e.** $60 **f.** $35 **5a.** 63 **b.** 28 **c.** 42 **d.** 160 **Fractions
and Patterns: 1a.** 3.27 **b.** 4.38 **c.** 5.42 **d.** 2.06 **2a.** 1 ¼ ,1 ½, **b.** 1.1, 1.3 **c.** 3.75, 4.25 **d.** 1.04, 1.00
3a. 2/8 OR ¼ ; 3/8; ½ OR 4/8; 5/8; **b.** 2/10 or 1/5; 4/10 OR 2/5; 7/10; 10/10 OR 1; **4.** order - 0.3, ½,
0.7, 4/5, 1.25, 1 3/5, 1.9, 2.2 **Faces & Nets: 1.** match : **a-g, b-h, c-f, d-e; 2. a.**□**b.**▲**c.**▽**d.**● **3a.**
cylinder **b.** rectangular prism **c.** cube **d.** cone **Location: 1.**

2. a.  **b.** 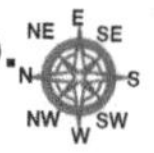 **c.**

3a. C2 **b.** G4 **c.** B5 **d.** I2 **e.** J5 **f.** E3 **g.** B1
h. H3 **i.** F1 **j.** D4 **k.** A3 **l.** C6 **m.** F6 **n.** J1 **o.** G2

Answers

Unit 24

Decimals and Percentages: 1a. ½ OR 5/10 OR 50/100 **b.** 2/5 OR 4/10 OR 40/100
c. 75/100 OR ¾ **d.** 90/100 OR 9/10 **e.** 1/10 OR 10/100 **f.** 8/100 **2a.** 2.5 **b.** 3.25 **c.** 1.8
3a. 19% **b.** 32% **c.** 84% **d.** 70% **e.** 50% **f.** 75% **4a.** $35 **b.** $90 **5a.** 60 **b.** 15 **c.** 48 **d.** 45 **e.** 14 **f.** 36
+ and − Fractions: 1a. 2/4 **b.** 4/10 **c.** 4/8 **d.** 8/10 **e.** 3/5 **f.** 2/3 **2a.** 4/8 **b.** 4/10 **c.** 5/9 **d.** 4/6
e. 6/10 **f.** 3/5 **3a.** 4/10 **b.** 6/8 **c.** 2/4 **d.** 3/9 **e.** 8/10 **f.** 4/6 **g.** 6/10 **h.** 2/8 **i.** 3/12
4a. 4/6+1/6=5/6 **b.** 4/10+3/10=7/10 **c.** 5/8+2/8=7/8 **d.** 3/8+4/8=7/8
Symmetry: 1. colour - **a, c, e, f, g, i** **2a.** 4 **b.** 5, parent check **3a.** ⬡ **b.** ⬡
4. triangles, squares, octagons
Data: 1a. 20 **b.** Sunday **c.** 35 **d.** 35 **e.** 345 **f.** $1 725 **2.**

Vanilla	5	10	15	1	16
Caramel	5	4			9
Chocolate	5	10	15	20	20
Strawberry	5	10	3		13

Unit 25

Calculator & Patterns: 1a. 12 396, 37 188, 111 564, **b.** 58 413, 58 420, 58 427 **c.** 36, 49, 64,
d. 10 663, 14 479, 18 295, **e.** 7 684, 7 337, 6 990, **f.** 13.28, 1.328, 0.1328 **2a.** 111, 120, 360, 40,
20, 480, 50, 25 **3a.** 185 **b.** 236 **c.** 564 **d.** 148 **e.** 216 **f.** 41 **4a.** 9.72 **b.** 14.24 **c.** 3.228 **d.** 0.38 **e.** 7.0
f. 1.132 **5a.** 0.5 **b.** 0.2 **c.** 0.8 **d.** 0.25 **e.** 0.625 **f.** 0.75
Multiplication: 1a. 918 **b.** 1 104 **c.** 1 512 **d.** 1 875 **e.** 1 792 **f.** 1 701 **g.** 2 413 **h.** 5 640
2a. $1 512 **b.** 9 216 apples **3.** Across - **1.** 72 **3.** 81 **5.** 88 **6.** 35 **10.** 8 **11.** 308
Down - **1.** 72 **2.** 18 **4.** 18 **6.** 32 **7.** 63 **8.** 90 **10.** 85
Circles: 1a. 10mm **b.** 15mm **c.** 20mm **2a.** 60mm **b.** 30mm **c.** 40mm **3.** Parent
24 Hour Time: 1a. 23:40 **b.** 19:10 **c.** 22:35 **d.** 13:25 **e.** 15:37 **2a.** 14:15 **b.** 01:10 **c.** 00:00
d. 22:55 **3a.** 10am **b.** 1:50pm **c.** 3:08am **d.** 12:05pm **e.** 12am **f.** 2:55pm
4a. 11:50 **b.** 13:00 **c.** 19:30 **d.** 00:15 **e.** 23:30

Unit 26

Credit Cards: 1. Might include: food, clothing, petrol, meals, theme park tickets, On-line goods and
so on… **2a.** 7539 1234 5678 4321 **b.** MyBank **c.** Ms G M I Good **d.** Wireless or WiFi **e.** 08/20
3. Parent. Any combination of 6 numbers **4.** monthly **5.** Possible answers: amount owing, date due
for payment, account number, statement period, credit limit, available credit, next statement end dat
Awards points, minimum payment due, name and address, account balance, all transactions for
past month **6.** Interest is charged daily on balance owing. **7.** An additional cost on borrowed money.
Division: 1a. T **b.** T **c.** F **d.** T **e.** F **f.** F **2a.** 120 r 7 **b.** 223r1 **c.** 125r2 **d.** 170r3 **e.** 71r1 **f.** 121r4
3a. 85 **b.** 82 **c.** 12 **d.** 22r3 **e.** 88 **f.** 5 **4a.** 626r4 **b.** 734r4 **c.** 725r1 **d.** 1 328r3 **e.** 591r2 **f.** 564r2
3D Objects: 1. Square pyramid **2.** Cone **3.** Hexagonal prism **4.** Cylinder **5.** Hexagonal pyramid
6. Cube **7.** Triangular prism **8.** Pentagonal prism **9.** Sphere **10.** Square pyramid
Location: 1. Samson Sports Ground **2.** Post Office **3.** Golf club **4.** P12-13 **5.** Underpass
6. N-S **7.** NE **8.** J1-2 **9.** Hospital **10.** E-W **11.** North **12.** Car park

Unit 27

Factors: 1a. colour - 63,28,49,21,91 **b.** colour - 36,81,90,27,54 **2a.** 81 **b.** 48 **c.** 84 **d.** 35 **e.** 55 **f.** 39
g. 48 **h.** 51 **3a.** 1,3,5,15 **b.** 1,2,3,4,6,8,12,24 **c.** 1,2,4,8,16 **d.** 1,2,4,7,14,28 **4a.** T **b.** T **c.** T **d.** T **e.** T
f. T **5a.** 16, **b.** 20 **c.** 36
Addition: 1a. 16 044 **b.** 16 249 **c.** 13 597 **2a.** 2 867 **b.** 1 696 **c.** 3 277 **d.** 15 410 **3a.** 10 517, 7 792
11 668 **b.** 14 408, 11 683, 15 559 **c.** 11 388, 8 663, 12 539 **d.** 9 519, 6 794, 10 670 **4a.** 14 000,
14 173 **b.** 11 000, 11 146 **c.** 16 000, 16 064 **5a.** $4 186.03 **b.** $8 441.22
Mass: 1a. gram **b.** tonne **c.** kilogram **d.** gram **d.** tonne **e.** gram **2a.** 944 grams **b.** 443 grams
c. 750 grams **3a.** 275g **b.** 167g **c.** 512g **d.** 1.265kg
Transformation: 1.a. ➡⬅⬆ **b.** 🌲◿◺ **c.** ⬗⬖◗

2.a. ◻ **b.** ⬖ **c.** ◆ **d.** ⬣

3a. flip **b.** turn **c.** slide

Unit 28

Place Value: 1a. 13 221 **b.** 25 041 **c.** 40 253 **2a.** 12 467 **b.** 12 578 **c.** 02 356 **d.** 12 378 **e.** 12 345
f. 00578 **3a.** 43 403 **b.** 70 353 **c.** 35 424 **4a.** tenths **b.** hundredths **c.** thousands **d.** ones **5a.** 70
b. 3 000 **c.** 700
Adding & Subtracting Decimals: 1a. 830.63 **b.** 634.28 **c.** 1 433.45 **2a.** 423.32
b. 531.14 **c.** 63.99 **3a.** 432.87 **b.** 778.65 **c.** 607.18 **d.** 1 267.92 **4a.** 654.96 **b.** 137.89 **c.** 418.14 m
5a. 20 mins 56 sec **b.** 151 metres **Angles: 1.a.** ∟ **b.** ∢ **c.** ∠ **2a.** 70° **b.** 100° **c.** 135° **d.** 25°
3a. 60° **b.** 81° **c.** 90°

4. a. 🎯 **b.** 🎯 **c.** 🎯 **d.** 🎯

5. 90°C **6.** 180°C **Measuring Time: 1a.** 6hrs 20mins **b.** 12hrs 38mins **c.** 8hrs 40 mins
2a. 04:32:19 **b.** 07:53:62 **c.** 10:19:48 **d.** 01:38:90 **3.** Two minutes, 27 seconds, 52 hundredths
4. 6:19:27, 7:14:33, 8:14:32, 8:40:36 **5.** 3:13:37 **6.** 7 hundredths of a sec.